How to Write Your Autobiography

Writing and Organizational Skills

by

Katherine Roberts Berndes

DISPLAYS FOR SCHOOLS, INC.
1825 N.W. 22nd Terrace
Gainesville, Florida 32605-3957

Copyright © 1997

All rights reserved. No part of this book may be reproduced or transmitted in any form or by any means, electronic or mechanical, including photocopying, recording, or any information storage and retrieval system, without permission in writing from the publisher.

ISBN: 0-9600962-6-4

I dedicate this book lovingly
to my son, Hans A. Berndes, MD
and
to my mother, Katherine J. Roberts
to my sister, Beverly R. Kearney

and in memory of my father
Allen C. Roberts

Also by Katherine R. Berndes

How to Write A Personal Narrative
How to Become A Better Consumer

TABLE OF CONTENTS

PREFACE IX

PART I   FIVE STEPS IN THE WRITING PROCESS 1

Introduction 2
1 PLAN 3
Chose A Topic - Earliest Memory 3
Recall And Collect Information 4
Narrow Down The Topic 5
List Ideas 6
Arrange Ideas In Sequential Order 8
Lead That Attracts Attention 9
Choose A Concise Title 11
Write The Ending 12

2 DRAFT 13
Write The First Draft 13
Evaluate The First Draft 14
Write The Second Draft 15

3 REVISE 16
Sentences 16
Paragraph Coherence 18
Paragraph Coherence - Transitional Words 19
Overworked Words 20
Repetitive Words 21
Concrete Details 22
Clichés 23
Vivid Words - Colors 24
Vivid Words - Size 25
Vivid Words - Taste And Smell 26
Vivid Words - Sound 27
Vivid Words - Texture And Feel 28
Interesting Conversation 29
Figurative Speech 30

4 EDIT 31
Spelling, Mechanics And Usage 31
Rules For Capital Letters 33
Rules For Punctuation 35

5 PUBLISH 41
Options 41
Simple Bookbinding 42

Manuscript Format	44
How To Write A Cover Letter	46
Mailing The Manuscript	47
Appropriate Markets	48
Record Of Submissions	49
Legal Rights	50

PART II ORGANIZATION 51

6 CHRONOLOGICAL ORDER 52

Genealogy Chart	54
Grandparents	55
Maternal Grandmother	55
Maternal Grandfather	56
Paternal Grandmother	57
Paternal Grandfather	58
Family	59
Mother	59
Father	60
Brother	61
Sister	62
Life Story	63

    Youth

Earliest Memory	Toys
Parents	Sports
Family Life	Recreation
Siblings	Vacations
Appearance	Music And Dance
Religion	Skills
Holidays	Personality
Foods And Beverages	Character
Economics	Pets
Emotional Intelligence	Milestones
Intelligence	The Arts
Education	Politics
Homes	Happy Times
Friends	Sad Times
Health	Feelings
	Future Plans

Stages Charts	98

7 COMPARISON OF STAGES 111
Comparisons	112

8 CAREER 113
Occupation	114

9 CULTURAL CHANGES 115
    The Arts   *Medicine*
    Architecture   *Music And Dance*
    Economic   *Politics*
    Education   *Population*
    Entertainment   *Recreation*
    Family Structure   *Transportation*
    Fashions   *Travel*
    Foods And Beverages   *Religion*
    Health   *Social Issues*
    Language   *Society's Values*
    Literature   *Values Charts*
                                         Comparison Of Societies

10 HISTORICAL EVENTS 144
    World War I 145
    Roaring Twenties 146
    The Great Depression 148
    World War II 149
    Atomic Age 150
    Korean War 151
    The Sixties 152
    Civil Rights 153
    Space Age 154
    War In Vietnam 155
    Persian Gulf War 156
    Other Countries 157

11 HOBBIES 158
    Collection 159
    Items In Collection 160

12 HOMES 161
    Homes In Your Country 162
    Homes In Foreign Countries 164

13 HUMOR 166
    Favorite Humorists 167
    Kinds Of Humor 169
    Humorous Experiences 171

14 JOURNAL 172
    Journal Entry 174

15 LETTERS 175

- Natural Abilities
- Comparison With Parents
- Comparison With Siblings
- Comparison With Children
- My Best Decision
- My Worst Decision
- I Wish That I Had . . .
- Most Exciting Experience
- Most Frightening Experience
- Funniest Experience
- Best Learning Experience
- Happiest Time
- Saddest Time
- Best Day
- Worst Day
- Favorite Hobbies
- Most Beautiful Sight
- Most Memorable Sight
- Friends At Different Stages
- Most Influential Person
- People I Have Admired
- Difficult People In My Life
- My Favorite Place
- Philosophy Of Life
- Best Advice
- Apology Letter
- Trips I Have Enjoyed
- How I See Myself
- How I Would Change Myself
- How I Would Change My Life
- Plans To Change My Community
- Plans To Change The World
- Contributions To Humanity
- Plans For The Future

16 PHOTOGRAPHY 210
- Selection Of Photos 211
- Description 214

17 POETRY 215
- Poems 216

18 THEME 217
- Choosing A Theme
- Chapters
- Travel
- Destinations

19 ECLECTIC 223
- Organization Of Information 224

20 AUTO-VIDEO TAPE 225
- Genealogy Chart 228
- Grandparents
  - Maternal Grandmother
  - Maternal Grandfather
  - Paternal Grandmother
  - Paternal Grandfather
- Family
  - Mother
  - Father
  - Sister
  - Brother
- Life Story
  - Birth
  - Childhood
  - Teenage Years
  - Education
  - Early Adult Years
  - Adult Life
  - Retirement
  - Evaluation Of Life
  - Future Plans

BIBLIOGRAPHY 246
APPENDIX 247

PREFACE

Have you always wanted to write the story of your life and didn't know where to begin? This workbook was planned to help writers, of all ages, improve their writing skills and organize information and mementos into a book. It is a concise, sequential and easy-to-follow reference for your entire family.

Writing narratives about events when you experience them is much easier than trying to remember how you felt about what happened years later. At the same time it reduces stress and improves your health. Your life story can be written any time; start writing today.

The ideas, lessons and writing skills are clear, concise and appropriate for every grade level, from the time students can write in the elementary grades, through high school, college, adult and lifelong learning programs. Students of all ages can write letters, journal entries, poetry, research family history, interview grandparents, do encyclopedia research, make an annual Auto-Video tape, take photographs, write travel articles about vacations and type narratives on a computer or typewriter. It is an important on-going English unit and lifelong writing project, a valuable tool for educators.

However, if you were not motivated to write your story in school, it's never too late to begin your book. You may have more time to spend on writing and be more interested at this stage of your life. This text helps you to improve your writing skills and suggests ways to organize your life story. It is self-explanatory, just answer the questions and follow directions.

Part I explains the five steps in the writing process: **Plan, Draft, Revise, Edit,** and **Publish**. Use them for the remaining stories in your autobiography and all other writing projects. Additional writing skills can be found in the text: *How to Write a Personal Narrative*, written by Katherine Berndes and published by Displays for Schools, Inc.

Part II suggests a variety of options for organizing your information. Chronological order is one method. This is your life story from birth on, including youth, teenage and adult years plus retirement. Maybe you enjoy writing letters, then why not write a series of letters to a favorite relative or friend? Add letters written to you. Are you an observer of cultural trends, or a historian? It's possible to trace these trends throughout history, while writing your life story. Do you have a special hobby? Have you been collecting baseball cards, stamps, toys, cars, or dolls? Cook books trace changes in foods and attitudes about eating and health. Books from other cultures reflect their values.

Photography is an excellent way to tell a story. Write about each picture. The whole story is there, just add your feelings. Have you got a sense of humor? Then why not write stories about funny experiences in your life? Are you a poet? Do you express your feelings in verse? Put your poems together for an autobiographical, poetic anthology. Have you been writing a daily journal? These entries can become your book, or part of it.

Did you live in interesting homes and places? They, too, can be another theme for your story. Trace the changes in your profession through the years. They can tell the story of your life and the history of the country. Was there one phase of your life that stands out in your memory? Maybe you were a country doctor, in a war, part of a revolution, or involved in another important social or political historic event. These themes can be the topic of a book. You can weave in the rest of your life story. Or, be eclectic, use all of these ideas to organize your memoirs.

No matter what organizational pattern you chose, have fun writing, and be creative. Remember it's an endless story; when you win a prize, get your name in the paper, have a new grandchild or take a trip, just add it to your book. Use old photographs, newspaper stories and mementos to refresh your memory. They make it more interesting.

Do additional research to add to your recollections. For example, if you are describing the Great Depression, read about it in a history book and interview people who lived in that era.

Plan a video tape of your present life and add others to your collection (marriage ceremony, baptism, football game). It becomes a visual record of your voice, appearance and personality - another dimension of you. It, also, gives you an opportunity to show and describe three-dimensional objects.

The book is in you, it should reflect your feelings, as well as actions. This text is a guide for writing your story. It contains specific questions to recall experiences that evoke mental pictures, which in turn elicit feelings and the circumstances surrounding the event. Think about the questions and answer them honestly. They are the outline for your narrative.

If you need more help, family members will be happy to help you recall the details that you have forgotten. Interview them by phone or in person. Request a tape with answers to your specific questions and other memorabilia that they might be willing to share.

In addition to the help you get from relatives, you will need to do research about your family history. Write and travel to places where your parents and grandparents were born and back to the countries where other ancestors originated. Visit the archives for information and interview people who knew them.

Contact the Superintendent of Documents, U.S. Printing Office, Washington, D.C. 20402 for *A Guide To Genealogical Records in the National Archives.* There is also an extensive genealogical library in Salt Lake City, Utah and branches throughout the United States. They can help you locate important information: copies of birth, marriage, and death certificates, real estate documents and discharge papers.

Adding your photographs, awards, newspaper articles, and other memorabilia will make the narratives more interesting. Store them in folders titled: Family History, Birth, Youth, Teenage Years, Adult Life and Retirement. These are chapters of your book.

When you type the narratives, leave 1 1/2 spaces between lines, a 1 inch margin on the left and a 1/2 inch margin on the right, 3/4 inch on the top and bottom of the pages. Type the page numbers at the top right corner or at the bottom of each page. Vary the type, according to the nature of the story. Illustrate the pages. Be consistent.

The newest duplicating machines can change sizes and copy photographs in color. Take them out of the frames and reproduce them. Give the photo a title, if you have decided not to write a narrative about it and explain the time, place and what was happening. Use it for the theme of a story. A photo of you on a pony when you were young might suggest a narrative, "I Always Wanted a Horse." If you write poetry, add humor, then paint or sketch pictures on the pages. All of these creative additions will make your narratives more interesting to read.

Give your book an appropriate short title. Then design an artistic cover. Arrange a collage of photos of all stages in your life or choose a single photograph and laminate it. After careful editing, you can have it reproduced for relatives and friends. There are directions for publishing and binding in Part I of this book. *The Writer's Market* will help you locate an appropriate publisher if you want to share it with a larger audience.

Writers need self-discipline. You learn to write by experience; write one or two pages every day at a designated time. Choose a quiet time free from all disturbances. In addition to this book, the following materials will be helpful: *Roget's Thesaurus,* a modern dictionary, an English handbook, information from relatives and your notes.

Read newspapers, magazines, poetry books and well-written autobiographies. Notice why they are popular. Keep a collection of good leads and writing styles. Subscribe to writing journals; they list workshops, markets, and help authors improve their writing skills. Writing workshops are also valuable learning experiences. Study photography and poetry. Become an expert in genealogy.

Become involved with other writers. They help critique your work. Take adult education and college courses that will improve typing and writing skills.

If you don't own a computer, study the newest technology. Take a course, join a computer club and learn from other members.

Narrowing down the topic and editing are the most difficult parts of writing. In this book the topics have been narrowed down; however, editing will need time and patience.

Write in your own voice, that is as you would speak. Just as you write better about topics you know and care about, writing as you think and speak makes it easier. It gives validity to your work.

In addition to telling your life story, writing an autobiography provides endless possibilities for personal growth and better health. It also encourages creativity, develops new skills and motivates travel. New friends and a better understanding of "who you are" and what motivated your behavior are additional benefits. Plus, there are opportunities for purifying emotions (catharsis), and strengthening the immune system. Aren't these excellent reasons for spending your time and energy on this writing project?

For most authors, writing is hard work, time consuming and often frustrating. However, it is a rewarding hobby that will fill many leisure hours and give you and your family a personal documentary that will be enjoyed for generations.

Follow directions, be creative and enjoy your writing journey into the past, present and future.

PART I

FIVE STEPS IN THE WRITING PROCESS

PLAN

DRAFT

REVISE

EDIT

PUBLISH

INTRODUCTION

Do you want to learn how to write more effectively? Part One of this book guides you, the author, through the five steps in the writing process: PLAN, DRAFT, REVISE, EDIT and PUBLISH. The directions have been planned to provide the writing foundation for this book and all other writing projects. Follow them, they are the tools for writing effectively.

The first step is to plan your narrative. The easiest way to begin writing your life story is to write about ONE experience. The question, "What was your earliest memory?" chooses the topic and narrows it down. **Step One**, narrowing down the topic, is the most difficult part. You are not writing the entire book at one time, but a small section of your life story. That's why it is so important to practice on one memory, not ALL your childhood memories.

Drafting, **Step Two,** and revising, **Step Three,** are the writing and rethinking steps. The rough draft is the first attempt to write down your ideas. Let them flow. Revision is essential and the key to good writing. It is the rethinking and reworking of the piece.

Editing, **Step Four**, is proofreading. It takes time and patience because the goal is perfection. Look for spelling, mechanical and usage errors.

Step Five is publishing. It is the creation of a book. You can bind it yourself, self-publish or attempt to locate an appropriate publisher. It can be enjoyed by you, your family and friends or with a wider audience.

Your book will be composed of many narratives, each one about **one** aspect of your life story. After you have completed this process for the first piece in your autobiography, the second part of this book will help you organize the way that you write the rest of this exciting story of your life.

1

PLAN

Choose A Topic - Earliest Memory

Recall your earliest memory. Try to remember how you felt at that time. Write it in one sentence.

I have many early memories. I believe my earliest memory is from when I was around 6 mos. old. I recall looking at my hand while riding in my carseat. I was wearing something pink which had "cover-ups" for my hands to fit into. My hand had come out and I was trying to get it back in, but couldn't. I felt enormously frustrated.

My feelings about the experience.

I described this scene to my mother and watched her eyes grow large as she said, "You couldn't have been more than 6 mos. old when you had that pink snowsuit." I find it interesting that my earliest memory is one of frustration at not being able to do something for myself + not being able to communicate my needs to those around me.

Find a photograph or draw a sketch to help you recall all the details.

Recall And Collect Information

First refresh your memory with photos, postcards, or discussions with others. Think about your feelings and attitudes about the topic. Share everything you remember about the subject with a partner who will record your ideas on this page. If you are working alone, record your ideas on a tape. Then answer these questions with phrases.

WHO was involved?
_____
_____

WHAT happened?
_____
_____
_____

WHERE did it happen?
_____
_____

WHEN did it happen?
_____
_____

WHY did it happen?
_____
_____

HOW did it happen?
_____
_____

HOW did you feel about it?
_____
_____

Narrow Down The Topic

Narrowing down the topic is the most important and most difficult part of writing a narrative. You have narrowed down the topic by choosing to write about ONE memory. Writing about all your earliest memories would be very difficult. Breaking down a topic of the Youth Stage information into small sections (birth, appearance, etc.), sometimes called narratives, is the goal of writing an autobiography that is organized and easy to both write and read.

If you do not stay within the guidelines of one topic, your narrative will lack unity and there will be no ending. Your essays and journal entries should have a beginning and end.

Titles and topics for all stages of your life have been suggested in PART II. If you use them for the remainder of your narratives, your autobiography will be organized and easy to read. With practice, you will eventually learn how to narrow down any topic and know when you have deviated from the subject. Write a theme for each story.

If you need additional help with choosing and narrowing down a topic, refer to *How to Write a Personal Narrative*, Katherine Berndes, STEP 1 - PLAN.

Write a theme for your earliest memory. (One sentence explaining it.)

_____
_____
_____
_____
_____
_____
_____

List Ideas

After discussing the topic or taping the experience, list all the ideas that you can remember about your first memory. Use phrases not sentences. Then delete all the ideas that are irrelevant. Ask the question: Is this related to my earliest memory?

In addition, get help from relatives that were with you. Locate photos or other memorabilia that will help you to recall all the events that took place at that time. Other information will evoke more stories about your youth.

Try to remember your feelings. Add things you saw, felt, heard, touched or tasted and smelled. These help to create word pictures.

SAW _____
_____
_____

FELT _____
_____
_____

HEARD _____
_____
_____

TASTED _____
_____

SMELLED _____
_____

TOUCHED _____
_____
_____

Think about the events, or ideas associated with your narrowed-down topic. Write one idea on each line, then transfer these ideas to 3" x 5" cards (one idea per card).

_____
_____
_____
_____
_____
_____
_____
_____
_____
_____
_____
_____
_____
_____
_____
_____
_____
_____
_____
_____
_____
_____
_____
_____
_____
_____
_____
_____
_____
_____

Arrange Ideas In Sequential Order

As you arrange the cards in sequential order, eliminate the ideas that aren't related to your topic. Copy the ideas down on this page according to when they happened. Write phrases; sentences are not necessary.

BEGINNING	MIDDLE	END
_____	_____	_____
_____	_____	_____
_____	_____	_____
_____	_____	_____
_____	_____	_____
_____	_____	_____
_____	_____	_____
_____	_____	_____
_____	_____	_____
_____	_____	_____
_____	_____	_____
_____	_____	_____
_____	_____	_____
_____	_____	_____
_____	_____	_____
_____	_____	_____
_____	_____	_____
_____	_____	_____
_____	_____	_____
_____	_____	_____

Lead That Attracts Attention

What is the first picture you want your reader to see? The lead is the most important part of the narrative. It should motivate the reader to read on. Write more than one lead using the following examples:

QUESTION *Why did the room feel so cold?*

_____
_____
_____
_____

SUSPENSE *The figure in the room was tall. His loud voice made me want to run away, but I was frozen to the floor.*

_____
_____
_____
_____

DESCRIPTION *Blood ran down my heel as I stepped on the piece of jagged glass.*

_____
_____
_____
_____

HUMOR *Everyone in the room was laughing, but I couldn't remember why.*

_____
_____
_____
_____

Do not start your first narrative with a statement that your first memory was . . . Experiment with other leads:

_____
_____

Write an opening paragraph for your two best leads:

LEAD

_____
_____
_____
_____
_____

LEAD

_____
_____
_____
_____
_____

Now decide which lead is the better of the two. It should capture the interest of your audience.

_____

Why is it better? _____
_____

If neither of them is interesting, write another one.

_____
_____
_____
_____
_____
_____
_____
_____
_____
_____

Choose A Concise Title

A title should capture the essence of the narrative with a few choice words. Begin to think about short, appropriate titles and write them down. Continue to think about the title while you are writing the narrative. Remember a few, well-chosen words will attract the reader's attention.

1. _____

2. _____

3. _____

4. _____

5. _____

6. _____

Check the one that you like best.

Add good titles that you have seen in current magazines articles. Find ones that attracted your attention. Why did you like them?

_____
_____
_____
_____
_____

Write The Ending

The ending of a piece is just as important as the beginning. Don't leave the reader unclear about the outcome.

Is there a surprise or expected resolution?

Write two or more endings. Continue to revise the one that you like best.

_____
_____
_____
_____
_____
_____
_____
_____
_____
_____
_____
_____
_____
_____
_____
_____
_____
_____
_____
_____
_____

2

DRAFT

Write The First Draft

Write your first draft using the order on your note cards. Be sure that the lead attracts your reader's attention. Don't worry about your spelling, handwriting or punctuation. Just explore ideas.

GUIDELINES to follow:
    Sound like yourself.
    Keep it simple and clear. Don't ramble.
    Say what you mean to say.
    Avoid foreign languages, write in English.
    Avoid using clichés such as: *it all boils down to.*
    Avoid using: *rather, pretty, little, very, nice, come, said* and *go.*
    Use figures of speech sparingly.
    Make your nouns and verbs powerful.
    Don't use awkward adverbs, (*overly, muchly, tiredly*).
    Add dialogue where it is clear who is speaking.

Write the theme of the piece (a few sentences that summarize the piece). All the sentences in the story should relate to it.

_____
_____
_____
_____

Evaluate The First Draft

Before you revise your work, take a second look at what you have written. Maybe you can find a colleague who can help you evaluate your narrative. Read it aloud for clarity. Does it sound like you are talking?

_____
_____

Did you cover all the ideas on your note cards?
_____

Is this piece of writing about one specific subject? (Theme)
_____

Does the lead sentence make you want to read on? (Copy here.)
_____
_____

What are some examples of concrete details, or specifics? Copy three good sentences.
_____
_____
_____

Do you feel good about this piece of writing? Why?
_____

Do you want to continue to work on this narrative? Why?
_____

If you do not want to continue working on this narrative, this is the time to put it aside. Don't throw it away; maybe it will interest you at a later date. Write about another memory, or any topic in PART II - ORGANIZATION.

Write The Second Draft

When you have finished the first draft, put it away for a day or two. Then read it aloud, as if you didn't write it. Decide if the words reflect what you meant. If they don't, revise or change them until they do.

Write a second draft and continue working on it to produce a final draft.

_____
_____
_____
_____
_____
_____
_____
_____
_____
_____
_____
_____
_____
_____
_____
_____
_____
_____
_____
_____
_____
_____
_____

NOTES

3

REVISE

Sentences

Sentences are groups of words that express a complete thought. They are the heart of the piece; make them clear and concise and keep related words together. Cross out sentences that do not clarify the subject or the paragraph in a useful way. Combine ideas which are closely related in thought into one sentence. Ideas which are not related should be separated.

Squash can be played both indoors and outdoors. Tennis is also an indoor and outdoor game.
Squash and tennis are both indoor and outdoor games.

Try not to write monotonous short sentences.

Dad enjoys playing squash and tennis. Jim also likes these sports.
Dad and Jim both enjoy playing squash and tennis.

Use the active voice. It is more direct than the passive.

Active: I shall always remember the first time I saw the Statue of Liberty.
Passive: *The movie was seen by Dad and Jim.*

Capitalize the first word of each sentence and all proper names (persons, places or things). End each sentence with the correct punctuation mark.

Which sentences don't relate to or clarify the subject?
_____
_____

Copy down one sentence in this piece that combines related ideas.
_____
_____

Copy down another sentence that uses the active voice.
_____
_____

Find short sentences.
_____
_____

Find sentences that do not express a complete thought.
_____
_____

Rewrite sentences that do not sound right when you read them aloud.
_____
_____
_____
_____
_____
_____
_____

Paragraph Coherence

Paragraph coherence results from a correct arrangement of its parts. Indent the first word.

It may be any length, a single sentence or a longer passage. However, it develops only one idea. Each paragraph must have a topic sentence which explains what the group of sentences is about.

Every detail sentence in the paragraph should logically follow the sentence before it. The sentence may be arranged in any order.

- by **Space** (left to right, from center to outward)
- by **Time** (as events occurred)
- by **Impression** (general to specific, specific to general)
- by **Importance** (least to most)

Paragraphs need a beginning, middle and end.

Copy one paragraph in your piece and revise it until it follows these suggestions.

_____
_____
_____
_____
_____
_____
_____
_____
_____
_____
_____
_____

Paragraph Coherence

Transitional Words

Paragraph coherence is achieved with transitional words. They are connections between sentences.

I believe that Brad is right. However, the group disagreed with him.

Transitional words and the relationships they show.

    Contrast   but, get, however, although, still, though, on the other hand, nevertheless

    Addition   in addition, also, and, moreover, furthermore

    Time   next, second, first, then, finally, after, later, when, before, until, at the same time, a few days later

    Position   there, here, behind, around, next to, to the right of, up, down, close to

    Cause and Result   since, because, thus, as a result, therefore, consequently

    Manner or Method   thus, similarly, for example, in this way

    Condition   unless, until, if

Copy three transitional words that you used.

_____
_____
_____
_____

Overworked Words

Use synonyms or words with similar meanings, to make your descriptions more clear, exact, or more interesting to your audience.

Avoid overworked words: **nice, some, said, go, rather, pretty, little, very, great, swell, cute, awful** and **a lot**.

Use a thesaurus to locate more specific words.

Here are some better word choices; add your own to the list.

NICE	COME	SAID	GO
accurate	advance	announced	advanced
agreeable	appear	asked	depart
amiable	approach	declared	go on
attractive	arrive	explained	go forward
discerning	burst	inquired	leave
exact	derive	objected	move
fastidious	descend	ordered	proceed
finished	draw near	replied	progress
neat	happen	screamed	move along
pleasant	take place	shouted	travel
scrupulous	occur	suggested	vanish

Circle the overworked words that you used in your piece. Now choose more exact words. (Nice girl/agreeable girl)

_____

Circle words that appear more than once in a sentence and in paragraphs. Then rewrite the sentences to eliminate repetitions.

_____
_____
_____
_____

Repetitive Words

Circle words that appear more than once in a sentence and in paragraphs. Then rewrite the sentences to eliminate repetitions.

She was my childhood friend. She lived in Baltimore.
Mary was my childhood friend, who lived in Baltimore.

Copy paragraphs with repetitive words. Circle the repetitions and revise them.

Concrete Details

Provide your readers with word pictures. Descriptive words will make a statement more interesting and informative.

The round, yellow cake that mother baked was covered with rich, dark, chocolate frosting.

Copy one statement in your piece that needs more specific details.

_____
_____
_____
_____
_____
_____

Revision

_____
_____
_____
_____
_____

Other revisions

_____
_____
_____
_____
_____

Collect good word pictures in magazine articles, books and newspapers.

Clichés

Avoid using clichés because they don't create a word picture. It is more effective to use specific terms to describe activities.

Write more descriptive examples for the following:
All boils down to
_____
_____

More than meets the eye
_____
_____

Nutty as a fruitcake
_____
_____

Other examples
_____
_____

Copy down clichés that you used in your story.
_____
_____
_____
_____

Revisions
_____
_____
_____

Find clichés in current magazine and newspaper articles and rewrite them.

Vivid Words - Colors

Vivid words help to create good word pictures or concrete details. Use sense impressions of the person, object or event being described. Involve as many senses as you can and use specific words. Consult *Roget's II The New Thesaurus*, *Scholastic Dictionary of Synonyms, Antonyms, Homonyms* and *Webster's Collegiate Dictionary*.

Color--If you want vivid wording, use basic colors (Red, white, blue, black, green and yellow) sparingly. Consider more specific words such as: shiny, fluorescent, neon, intense, opaque, bleach, streaked, muddied, flame-like, or washed-out.

These are examples of how one color (blue) can be made more vivid: *powder blue, aquamarine, beryl, cobalt blue, eggshell blue, jouvence blue, marine blue, cerulean, indigo, azure, ultramarine*

BLUE	**RED**	**WHITE**	**BLACK**	**GREEN**	**YELLOW**
cobalt	crimson	cream	ebony	chartreuse	blond
indigo	ruby	flesh color	jet black	emerald	canary
marine blue	scarlet	ivory	raven	jade green	lemon
sky blue	vermilion	off-white	sable	olive	sulphur

Find examples of color word pictures in your piece and copy them down (Red dress/scarlet dress).

_____
_____
_____
_____
_____
_____
_____

Vivid Words - Size

Words such as *little* and *small*, *big* and *large* are not specific. Use them sparingly. Try to compare the size of unknown objects to ones familiar to the reader.

Consider these more vivid words for small and large.

LITTLE	**SMALL**	**LARGE**	**BIG**
brief	paltry	ample	gross
diminutive	petite	broad	hefty
dwarf	petty	bulky	husky
feeble	pygmy	capacious	immense
fine	scanty	colossal	important
illiberal	seldom	comprehensive	inordinate
inconsiderable	short	considerable	major
inferior	slender	copious	mammoth
insignificant	slight	cumbersome	monstrous
mean	smallish	fat	stupendous
minor	trivial	gargantuan	swollen
minute	weak	gigantic	towering
narrow	unimportant	great	voluminous

Circle words for size in your piece. Find better words for them. (Little trip/brief trip).

_____
_____
_____
_____
_____
_____
_____
_____
_____

Vivid Words - Taste And Smell

The most accurate method of describing a specific taste is to compare the taste or odor to some other well known taste or smell. Avoid words that indicate a judgment: good, bad, delicious, horrible, excellent or tasty.

Primary tastes are sweet, sour, salty and bitter. Tastes are a combination of smell and taste.

Consider these more descriptive words for the following words.

SWEET	SOUR	BITTER	SALTY
candied	acid	absinthe	brackish
dulcet	acerb	acrid	briny
fragrant	acetous	harsh	pungent
luscious	curdled	sharp	saline
nectareous	pungent	sour	sharp
saccharine	rancid	stinging	sodium
sugary	tart	tart	chloride

Circle words for taste and smell in your narrative and copy them down (*Sweet lemonade/sugary lemonade*).

___
___
___
___
___
___
___
___
___

Vivid Words - Sound

The words *loud* and *quiet* provide only general impressions of a sound. Describe sounds as to intensity (degree of volume) and to the kind and quality of sound. Metaphors are implied comparisons; they help to describe sounds. For example: *John is a canary in the shower.*

Consider these more descriptive words for the following.

INTENSITY OF SOUND	QUALITY OF SOUND
barely audible	barking
bellowing	buzzing
blaring	clinking
clamoring	crashing
earsplitting	growling
faint	gurgling
hushed	harmonious
muffled	humming
peeping	purring
piercing	raucous
shouting	rumbling
thunderous	swishing
whispering	tinkling

Circle the words in your piece that explain the intensity of sound and choose more descriptive ones. (*Loud scream/piercing scream*)

_____
_____
_____
_____
_____
_____
_____

Vivid Words - Texture And Feel

Words such as *hard* and *soft* or *rough* and *smooth* are not specific. They give the reader only a general impression of the texture.

Consider these more specific words.

ROUGH	ROUGH	HARD	SMOOTH	SOFT
bristly	pointed	bland	compact	fine
bumpy	prickly	even	dense	glossy
clammy	rocky	flat	firm	luxurious
coarse	rubbery	glassy	impenetrable	sleek
craggy	rugged	glossy	solid	smooth
gnarled	sandpaperish	plain		
grainy	sandy	plastic		
gritty	shaggy	polished		
icy	sticky	silky		
jagged	wrinkled	sleek		
mushy		suave		

Circle these words in your piece: *rough, hard, smooth, soft*. Find more specific words (S*mooth water/glassy water*).

_____
_____
_____
_____
_____
_____
_____
_____

Interesting Conversation

Write interesting conversation: *Mother predicted, "A hurricane will hit today."*

1. Quotation marks are used around the speaker's exact words.
2. A comma follows the part that introduces the exact words of a speaker. It appears outside the quotation.
3. The exact words of a speaker begin with a capital letter.
4. When the spoken words are at the end of a sentence, the period or the question mark goes inside the quotation marks.
5. The first word of a quotation is indented each time the speaker changes.

Try some other verbs instead of "said" in conversation. The sentence should match the type of verb you use.

mourned	whispered	roared	verbalized
begged	began	repleted	muttered
shrieked	asked	ranted	mumbled
screamed	raged	reminded	signed
sneered	taunted	greeted	declared
pleaded	teased	boomed	guessed
announced	hooted	snarled	invited
squeaked	fussed	accused	returned
howled	stammered	persisted	snapped
wondered	remembered	decided	retorted
spoke up	commanded	hesitated	stated
gasped	responded	murmured	breathed
prayed	wondered	chuckled	informed

Copy a dialogue in your story and revise it.

_____
_____
_____

Figurative Speech

Use these figures of speech when they are appropriate.

Simile is an explicit or direct comparison using the words *like* or *as*.
Brett swims like a fish.

Metaphor is an implied comparison.
Brett was a fish during the last swim meet.

Personification is attributing human qualities to inanimate objects.
The sun smiled through the clouds.

Hyperbole is an exaggeration for effect.
Brett is the finest and best swimmer in the world.

Onomatopoeia is the use of words whose sounds mirror their meanings. *Clang-clang, swish, splash, cuckoo.*

Identify these figures of speech:
eats like a bear _____
cat-like walk _____
stone face _____
clammy hands _____
cauliflower ears _____
gentle as a lamb _____
starry-eyed _____
stubborn as a mule _____
whale of an appetite _____
raven hair _____
Copy down examples of figurative speech. _____
_____
_____
_____
_____

NOTES

4

EDIT

Spelling, Mechanics And Usage

Use pages 31-40 to help you edit your narrative for errors in spelling, mechanics and usage. Also, the bibliography lists additional grammar references. Circle all words that are misspelled in your narrative. Use the dictionary or computer for correct spelling.

Words misspelled _____

EDITING GUIDELINES: Record your problems for future reference.

Capitalization (pages 33-34)	Yes	No
Proper nouns and I		
First words in sentence		
Title, abbreviations and initials		
Chapters in books, stories, poems, songs, reports		
Letters (greeting and closing)		
Copyrighted names		
First word of a formal statement following a strong interjection		

Punctuation (pages 35-37)

	YES	NO			YES	NO
Apostrophe '	___	___	Brackets **[ ]**		___	___
Comma ,	___	___	Parentheses **( )**		___	___
Colon :	___	___	Semicolon **;**		___	___
Dash —	___	___	Ellipsis **. . .**		___	___
Hyphen -	___	___	Question Mark **?**		___	___
Period .	___	___	Exclamation Pt. **!**		___	___
			Quotation Marks **" "**		___	___

	Yes	No
Underlining (page 40)		
Title of books, magazines, newspapers		
Foreign terms		
For emphasis or a subject of discussion		
Numerals (pages 39-40)		
Dates, page numbers, street numbers		
Decimals and percents		
Spell out numbers (one or two words), ages and hour of day		
Use symbols in statistics, technical, business and math writing		
Sentences (pages 16-17)		
Clear, concise and logical sequence		
No fragments or run-on sentences		
Variety of patterns		
Agreement of subject and predicate		
Appropriate transitional words		
Paragraphs (pages 18-19)		
Accurate and sequential		
Indent first word		
Topic sentence		
Overworked words (page 20)		
Avoidance of *nice, come, said, go, rather*		

Rules For Capital Letters

Capital letters are used for the following:

1. Names of proper nouns (Real or fictional), rivers, oceans, lakes, seas, bays, mountains and gulfs, colleges, schools, states, streets, avenues, roads, rural routes, towns, cities, geographical regions (*the North*) and the people who live there (*Northerners*), and continents

2. Names of proper adjectives:
    New York, New Yorker

3. Sacred documents and words referring to God and deities, the names of church, synagogues and religions:
    The Bible and its books

4. Names of races, nationalities, languages, countries and political parties:
    English, England, Republican

5. Names of newspapers, firms and organizations, ships, aircraft and spacecraft:
    Challenger

6. Names of the days of the week, holidays and months of the year:
    Thanksgiving is Thursday.

7. Names of persons and pets, mother, father when used as part of a person's name (*Uncle John*), or as a substitute for a person's name (*Ask Dad*) and the pronoun, *I*.

8. Titles (*Mrs. Jones*), abbreviations (*A.D.*), and initials (*J.J. Brown*).

9. Language subjects:
    Spanish, English, French

10. Historical events, periods and documents (*the Gettysburg Address*), buildings, parks and monuments (*Statue of Liberty*)

11. Copyrighted names, trademarks and brand names (*Jello*)

12. First word in a sentence:
    The letter arrived today.

13. First word in a line of poetry:
    I think that I shall never see . . .

14. First and most important words in the greeting of a letter (*Dear Uncle Joe*) and the first word in the closing of a letter (*Yours truly*)

15. First, last and important words in titles of English works and chapters of books, magazines, plays and motion pictures, stories, poems, songs, reports and art works

16. First word in main idea and subhead in outlines

17. First word following a strong interjection:
    Ouch! The fire is burning me.

18. In written conversation, the first word of the speaker:
    Mary remarked, "The day is sunny."

19. The first word of a formal statement or resolution following the introductory italicized words:
    Resolved, That the world has millions of starving people.

Rules For Punctuation

APOSTROPHE (')
An apostrophe is used to show possession:
> *dog's collar* (Singular - one dog) add '*s*
> *girls' dresses* (Plural - many girls) add '

An apostrophe is used to take the place of an omitted letter or letters (contraction):
> *it's* (it is)

An apostrophe is used to show the plurals of all small letters:
> *We were instructed to label by letters, the b's first, c's second, and d's third.*

An apostrophe is used for all capital letters with periods.
> *We were the first women to receive M.A.L.S.'s at a men's college.*

An apostrophe is used for all capital letters that would be confusing if *s* alone were added, add '*s*.
> *We checked the B's, U's and T's in the telephone directory.*

BRACKETS [ ]
Brackets are used to enclose explanations, comments and corrections that are inserted into a quotation from another author:
> *It was this poem ["The Iliad and the Odyssey"] that made Homer famous.*

Brackets are used as parentheses within parentheses:
> *The population is over 2 billion (see Appendix C [Chart V] on page 27).*

COLON (:)
The colon is a mark that directs attention to what follows. It has many uses: Introduces a list of items, a statement or question, a series of statements, or a long quotation. The words before it must be a grammatical sentence.
> *He bought the following books: English, psychology, social studies and health.*

After the greeting of a business letter:
> *Dear Mr. Baron:*

Between hours and minutes:
> *8:35 P.M.*

Between volume and page numbers of a magazine:
> *National Geographic 112: 100 - 127.*

Between a Biblical chapter and verse:
> *Matthew 2:6*

Separates the title and subtitle of a book:
> *Vietnam: The Causes and Results*

After a statement which is followed by an explanation:
> *John didn't care about the product's failure: none of his money was invested in it.*

COMMA (,)

A comma is used to separate a town from a state:
> *Salt Lake City, Utah*

A comma is used between the day of the month and year and after the year unless it is the last word in the sentence:
> *On Wednesday, August 6, 1986, we were on vacation.*

A comma is used to separate words, clauses or groups of words in a series:
> *Jack, Bill and Jake are my friends.*

Use a comma to set off words (name) in direct address:
> *"John, come to the table for dinner," demanded Mary.*

Use a comma to set off appositives:
> *The boy, a hyperactive teenager, coudn't sit still during the film.*

Use a comma after introductory words or clauses: *no, yes, oh, well*
> *No, I don't want a convertible car.*
> *While watching the skydiver, she wished that she had the courage to try the sport.*

Commas precede coordinating conjunctions that join main clauses:
> *I will go to the store today, and you can go to the beach.*

A comma follow the greeting of a personal letter and the closing of all letters: *Dear Jan, Very truly yours,*

DASH (—)
A dash indicataes a sudden break in a thought, or an unfinished statement:
> *The girl went there —where did she go?*

A dash is used before a summary or an appositive:
> *Jogging, exercising, dieting—all this she did to lose weight.*

ELLIPSIS MARK (...)
An ellipsis mark indicates halting speech or an omission in the sentence:
> *He stammered, "I'm really . . . I mean . . . like . . . very nervous."*

An ellipsis mark is used to indicate omitted words in a direct quotation:
> *"In the . . . heavens and earth." Genesis 1:1*

EXCLAMATION POINT (!)
An exclamation point is used at the end of a sentence to express strong feeling or emotion:
> *"Shoot!" the hunter ordered.*
> *What beautiful fireworks!*

HYPHEN (-)
A hyphen is used to join two or more words used as a compound adjective before a noun:
> *A well-timed remark.*
> *Heat-and-serve products.*

A hyphen is used when spelling numbers from twenty-one to ninety-nine and fractions used as modifiers:
> *He is thirty-one years old.*
> *The cup is one-half full.*

Use a hyphen when it is necessary to divide a word at the end of a line. Divide it between syllables and put the hyphen at the end of the line:
> *He placed an advertisement for his bicycle in the local news-paper.*
> *He is ex-President Hoover's relative.*

PARENTHESES ( )
Parentheses are used to enclose words apart from the main thought:
>*If you take the trip (and I do hope you will), be sure to bring your camera.*

Use parentheses to enclose words that are explanatory, exemplary, or supplementary.
>*Three members of the Club (Nan, Jan and Bonnie) were trying to win the tournament.*

Use parentheses to enclose symbols or letters in a series:
>*Jed had three choices: (1) to buy a car (2) take a trip to Hawaii or (3) save the money.*

PERIOD (.)
A period is used to end a sentence that makes a request or statement.
>*The doctor came to the house.* (declarative)

A period is used after abbreviations and initials:
>A. D.
>J. Brown
>A. M.

QUESTION (?)
A question mark is used at the end of a question:
>*Will she come?*

QUOTATION MARKS (" ")
Quotation marks are used to enclose titles of songs, chapters, articles, poems, stories and parts of musical compositions:
>*The article is entitled, "Coping With Stress."*

Enclose a direct quotation with quotation marks:
>*"You broke my crystal vase," she complained.*

Use quotation marks around fragmented conversation:
>*"I'm not so sure," she remarked, "that I have met you before."*

Use quotation marks around unacceptable or rarely used phrases, nicknames, or words (used ironically):
>*They are "boiling mad" about the deal.*

My old friend, "Shorty," came to see me.
His "mansion" was a hut in the woods.

SEMICOLON (;)

A semicolon is used to join two independent clauses not connected by *but, or, for,* or *and*:

The rain was so heavy; we had to stop the car.

Use a semicolon to separate independent clauses joined by conjunctive adverbs (*Nevertheless, however, consequently, accordingly, thus, then, therefore, hence*):

The morning was foggy; therefore, we postponed the picnic.

A semicolon precedes *as, namely,* or *thus* before introducing examples:

Four people were nominated; namely, Mona, Bruce, Ben and Lisa.

A semicolon is used between items in a series if any of the items contains a comma, and to prevent misreading:

The members of the Board of Education included Jane Barry, a homemaker; Brett Jones, an architect; and Dr. Van Dorn, a local physician.

NUMERALS

Write numerals for dates, page numbers, street numbers, decimals and percents:

Jamie lives at 12 Spanish River Court.
Jake got 50 percent of the votes.

Don't use $ for sums less than one dollar:

The yogurt cone cost ninety-five cents.

Spell out all round numbers if they can be written in one or two words:

He sold two thousand copies of the book.
There are 5,679 copies left to be sold.

Spell out a person's age, or the hour of the day:

Jan is eighteen years old.
It is three o'clock in the afternoon.

Don't begin a sentence with numerals. Write our the words:

Twenty-five students, or two-thirds of the student body, attended the rally.

Figures are generally used in technical, mathematical or business writing:
> *100 square feet*
> *4 1/4 percent*
> *8.9 meters*
> *$1.89 a pound*

Large numbers can be written with words or numerals:
> *3,670,223 people*
> *Four million dollars, 4 million dollars or $4,000,000*

UNDERLINING

Underline for emphasis:
> *He <u>would</u> return in spite of all the problems.*

Underline titles of books, magazines and newspapers:
> *I just read <u>Future Shock</u> by Alvin Toffler.*

CORRECTIONS

Make your revisions after editing. Put the work aside for a few weeks. Then read it aloud, or record it on a cassette tape. Play it back. Listen to the style, usage and content. Find your mistakes and list them.

1 _____

2 _____

3 _____

4 _____

5 _____

6 _____

Copy over your narrative with all the corrections. Your final copy should be perfect.

5

PUBLISH

Options

Now that your personal narrative is finished, the first thing to do is **enjoy it**, and then go on to the next one.

Illustrate the pages or add photographs and postcards.

How do you feel about it?
_____

Read it, and share it with friends, family, teachers and other authors.

Treat it as a **practice**.

Or, consider **publishing** it.

Do you read magazines or newspapers that might consider it for publication? _____

Do your friends, family and teachers like it?
_____

Are you willing to risk rejections? _____

Bind it into a book.

Simple Bookbinding

Materials:
- cardboard
- 12 sheets of lined or unlined white or wallpaper or fabric
- needle and nylon thread
- ruler
- compass
- wide tape
- scissors
- paper cutter

Decide on the following:
- Fabric or paper cover
- Size of the book
- Size and color of the paper for inside

Instructions for The Inside:
1. Fold 12 sheets of paper in half. Cut to desired size.
2. Mark 5 dots (evenly spaced) on the centerfold 3/4 inches from the top and bottom of the pages.

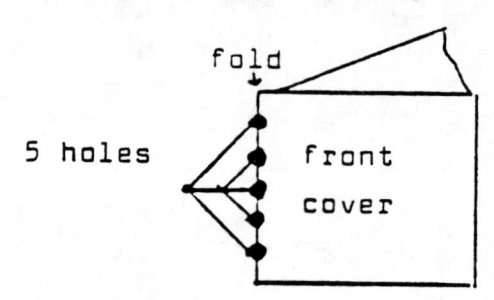

3. Use the compass to poke holes through the pages.
4. Sew through holes from top to bottom and back up again. (Use double thread.)

Instructions for the Cover:
1. Cut 2 pieces of cardboard ½ inch wider and 1 1/4 inch longer than the folded pages.

2. Cut 1 piece of cardboard 1/4 inch wide and the same length as the two sides.
3. Measure and cut a piece of wide tape 2 inches longer than the length of the cardboard.
4. Place cardboard pieces on tape. Leave enough space for the book to close. Fold the tape over.
5. Measure the opened cardboard book cover.
6. Cut the paper or fabric 3 1/4 inches wider and 2 ½ inches longer than the book cover.
7. Place the cover over the paper or fabric (center it). Leave 1 5/8 inches on each side (length) and 1 1/4 inches on the top and bottom.
8. Mark where the cover was placed. Remove the cover from the fabric or paper. Put glue on the back of the fabric or paper cover. Replace the cover and PRESS.

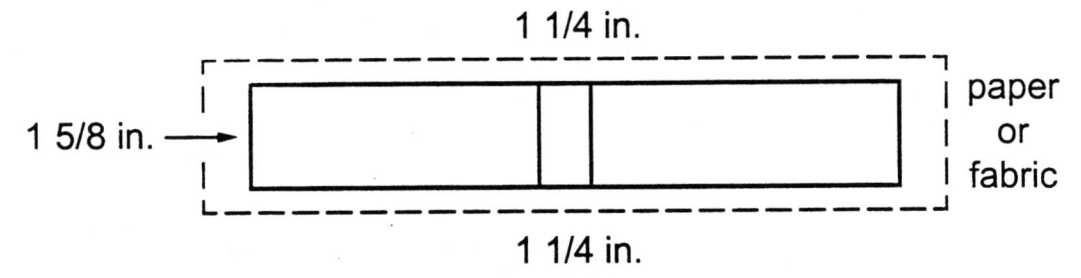

```
              1 1/4 in.
        ┌─────────────────────┐
        │   ┌───────┬───────┐ │  paper
1 5/8 in. →  │       │       │ │  or
        │   └───────┴───────┘ │  fabric
        └─────────────────────┘
              1 1/4 in.
```

9. Fold the four corners over the cardboard.

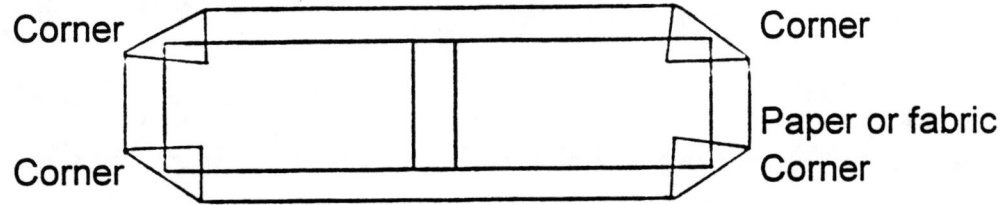

Corner ... Corner

Corner ... Paper or fabric Corner

10. Fold the top, bottom, and sides and glue them. (Fold it first to set and then glue)

Finishing the Book

1. Place the inside pages on the cover so that the centerfold (stitched part) rests in the center of the cover.
2. Glue the first page to the front cover and the last page to the back cover. When gluing the second cover, lift the cover to a 45° angle so that the cover will not be too tight.
3. Decorate the cover with embroidery or a collage of photos.

Manuscript Format

If you plan to submit a story, follow these directions:
Use large black pica type. Don't use script, italics, old English or all capitals.
Use 8 ½ " x 11" white paper - 25% cotton fiber and 20-pound bond.
Do not use erasable paper.
Type and edit the manuscript.

Your Name	Four	Approximately _____words
Street	Single	Rights offered
City, State, Zip Code	spaced	© Copyright 199___
	lines	Your name

1 1/4 "
Margin
on all
four sides

Halfway
Down the
Page

TITLE
(Center and Capitalize the Title)

Skip 3 double spaces.
    Indent all paragraphs five letter spaces. Always double space sentences. Do not divide works at the end of the line.

_____
_____
_____
_____
_____
_____
_____
_____

Don't staple the pages together (use paper clips).
Photocopy and save a copy of your personal narrative.
Estimate the approximate number of words to the nearest hundred words.
Pages are numbered on the top left-hand corner.

Page 2 of the manuscript goes on the left side of the page. Go down two spaces and continue typing the manuscript.

End the article after the last sentence, then skip three double spaces and center:

The End

Fold the manuscript:

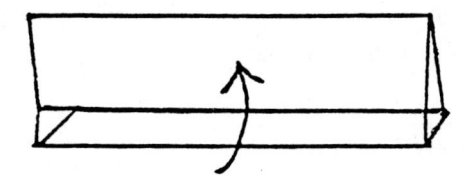

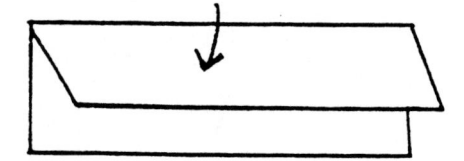

Mail it in a long envelope.

Enclose a stamped, self-addressed envelope (SASE).

How To Write A Cover Letter

Plan, write and neatly type a short business letter similar to this one. It should explain your personal narrative concisely. This letter will not sell your article, it only personalizes it. Be brief. This is a draft. Revise, edit and type it neatly.

	Your Street Your Town, State, Zip Code Month, Day, Year
Inside address If you do not know the editor's name write Dear Madam or Dear Sir.	Mr. John Brown, Editor Publishing Company Street City, State, Zip Code Dear
Writing Background	I am a writing teacher and published author of three books. I presently edit our condominium newsletter.
Qualifications for writing the eclosed narrative	Enclosed you will find four narratives that are part of my autobiographical story of our sailing trip around the world, *A Year At Sea.* They describe our unique experiences in stormy seas and among killer sharks. The book is a journal of our frightening, exciting and beautiful sights at sea. Enclosed is a SASE. Thank you for considering my story.
Closing and Signature (Script) Name	Yours truly, (title) Your Name

Mailing The Manuscript

Letter to the Publishing Company

```
Your Name                                          Stamp
Street                                             (Affixed)
City, State, Zip Code


                        Editor's Name
                        Publishing Company
                        Street
                        City, State, Zip Code
```

SASE - Letter Addressed to Yourself

```
                                                   Stamp
                                                   (Affixed)



                        Your Name
                        Street
                        City, State, Zip Code
```

Be sure to weigh the envelope before you mail it FIRST CLASS.

Appropriate Markets

If you decide to publish your piece, visit the library for appropriate markets. Many publishing companies will send you sample copies of their publications and writer's guidelines. This information will save you time and postage.

List the references:
LITERARY MARKETPLACE
_____
_____
_____

WRITER'S MARKET
_____
_____
_____

WRITER'S MAGAZINES
_____
_____
_____

Read the publications that are possible markets. Would your manuscript be appropriate? Don't send a personal narrative about a trip to Universal Studios to a sport magazine.

Choose five potential markets

Publisher	Address	What They Buy	Legal Terms	Payment Information	Other Information
1.					
2.					
3.					
4.					
5.					

Record Of Submissions

Send the perfectly typed manuscript with the SASE and the cover letter to the first publisher on your list. Wait until the editor responds before you send in the next submission.

Submit one manuscript at a time.

Title:_____

Date Sent	Publisher	$ Cost	Results	Income
1.				
2.				
3.				
4.				
5.				

Notes

_____
_____
_____
_____
_____
_____
_____
_____
_____
_____
_____
_____

Legal Rights

If the editor offers you a contract. Read it carefully. *The Writer's Market*, a book generally found in the public library, explains these rights:

One-Time Rights _____

First Serial Rights _____

Second Serial Rights _____

All Rights _____

Simultaneous Rights _____

Which rights were you offered? _____

If you don't understand the contract, ask the editor to clarify the legal language, or consult a lawyer. The copyright law protects your writing for fifty years after you death. As the author of your work, you have control over how it is used.

However, you can register the work with the Copyright Office. Send $20.00 to the Register of Copyrights, Library of Congress, Washington, D.C. 20559, along with a copy of the work you wish to copyright, and their form.

See *The Writer's Market* and other references for additional information about copyright procedures.

Did you decide to copyright your work?
_____

Why? _____

PART II

ORGANIZATION

CHRONOLOGICAL ORDER

COMPARISON OF STAGES

CAREER

CULTURAL CHANGES

HISTORICAL EVENTS

HOBBIES

HOMES

HUMOR

JOURNAL

LETTERS

PHOTOGRAPHY

POETRY

THEME

ECLECTIC

AUTO-VIDEO TAPE

NOTES

6

CHRONOLOGICAL ORDER

Writing your life story in chronological order is one way to organize your memories and reactions to your life into a book. That is, your life as you lived it or are living it.

Include mementos and family stories about your ancestors, youth, teenage, adult and retirement years. Give these stages of your life some thought before writing your impressions and include all the stages and topics. When contacting relatives about family information, send specific questions and a self-addressed stamped envelope for best results.

Once you have exhausted your personal search, try public records: county courthouses, historical societies, state archives, U.S. Census Bureau and the Mormon church. Don't forget churches and cemeteries. Your search may even lead you to foreign countries.

The questions about your youth have been planned to help you recall experiences and even feel them again. They will elicit both happy and sad memories, traumatic experiences, strong emotions and create mental pictures. These good, bad, happy and sad experiences are part of everyone's life. Be honest. Writing about them will help heal the wounds.

You can begin your autobiography, "My name is . . . I was born in the town of . . . The book suggests numerous ideas for beginning the story of your life. Organize your information and materials. Then write your story.

The last charts compare the stages in your life. Fill in the ideas, using the questions in the Appendix. Describe the remaining stages (Teen-age, Adult and Retirement) in your autobiography.

GENEALOGY CHART

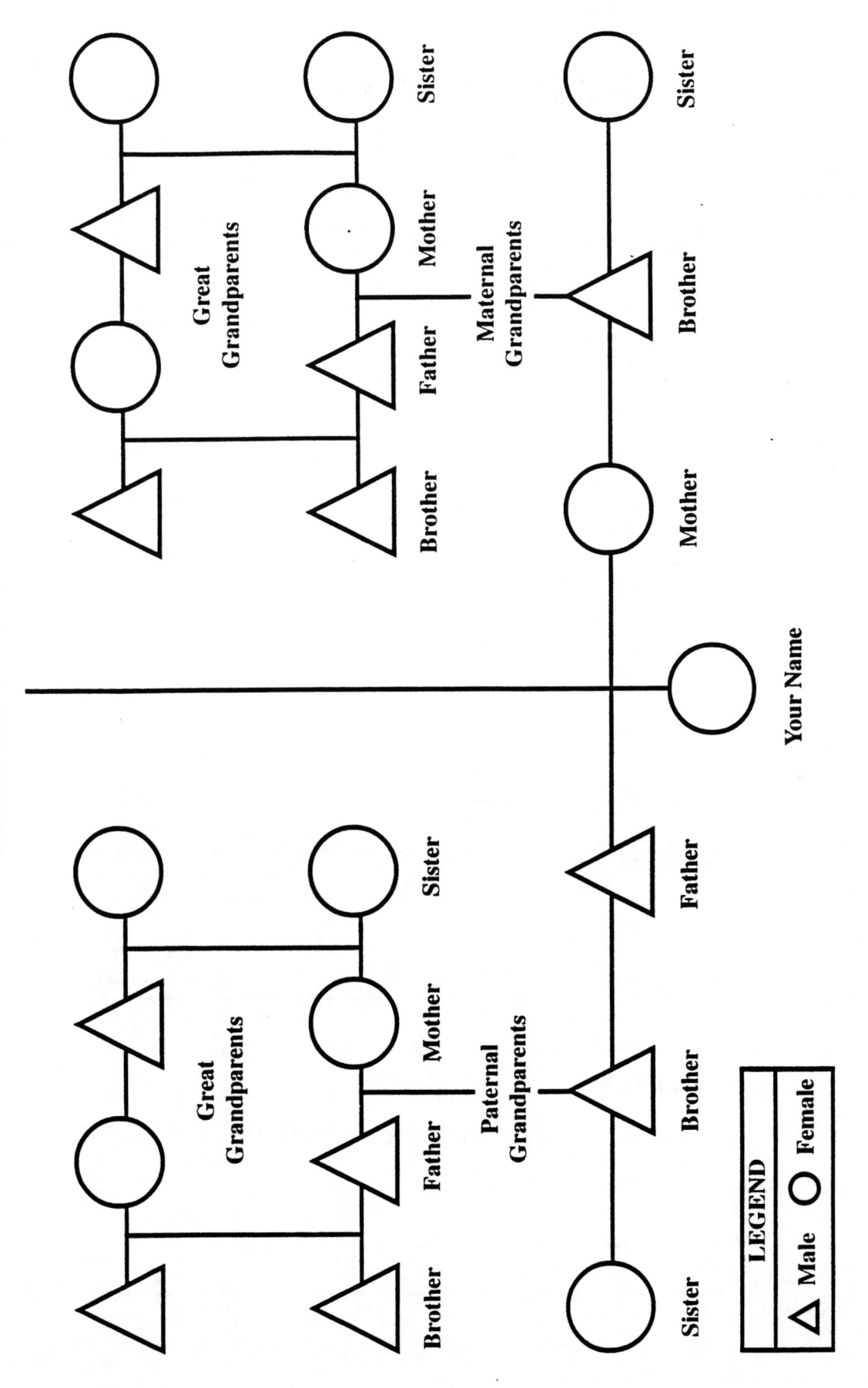

Great Grandparents

Great Grandparents

Brother — Father / Mother — Sister
Paternal Grandparents

Brother — Father / Mother — Sister
Maternal Grandparents

Sister — Brother — Father

Mother — Brother — Sister

Your Name

LEGEND
△ Male ○ Female

54

Grandparents

Maternal Grandmother

Grandmother on your mother's side of the family.

Name _____

Appearance _____

Age _____

Nationality _____

Personaity _____

Life story _____

_____

Birth: date, place _____

Youth _____

Education _____

Profession or trade _____

Married Life _____

Children _____

Interests _____

Contributions to the family _____

_____

Death: date, place, causes _____

If she left the country where she was born, explain the reasons and other facts about her place of origin.

_____

_____

Title _____

Theme _____

Grandparents

Maternal Grandfather

Grandfather on your mother's side of the family.

Name _____

Appearance _____

Age _____

Nationality _____

Personaity _____

Life story _____

_____

Birth: date, place _____

Youth _____

Education _____

Profession or trade _____

Married Life _____

Children _____

Interests _____

Contributions to the family _____

_____

Death: date, place, causes_____

If he left the country where he was born, explain the reasons and other facts about his place of origin.

_____

_____

Title_____

Theme _____

Grandparents

Paternal Grandmother

Grandmother on your father's side of the family.

Name _____

Appearance _____

Age _____

Nationality _____

Personaity _____

Life story _____

_____

Birth: date, place _____

Youth _____

Education _____

Profession or trade _____

Married Life _____

Children _____

Interests _____

Contributions to the family _____

_____

Death: date, place, causes_____

If she left the country where she was born, explain the reasons and other facts about her place of origin.

_____

_____

Title_____

Theme _____

Grandparents

Paternal Grandfather

Grandfather on your father's side of the family.

Name _____

Appearance _____

Age _____

Nationality _____

Personaity _____

Life story _____

_____

Birth: date, place _____

Youth _____

Education _____

Profession or trade _____

Married Life _____

Children _____

Interests _____

Contributions to the family _____

_____

Death: date, place, causes _____

If he left the country where he was born, explain the reasons and other facts about his place of origin.

_____

_____

Title _____

Theme _____

Family

Mother

Describe your mother. Add photographs.

Name _____

Appearance _____

Age _____

Nationality _____

Personaity _____

Life story _____

_____

Youth _____

Education _____

Profession or trade _____

Married Life _____

Children _____

Interests _____

Contributions to the family _____

_____

Your relationship to her _____

How were you similar to her? _____

How were you different from her? _____

If she left the country where she was born, explain the reasons and other facts about her place of origin.

_____

Title_____

Theme _____

Family

Father

Describe your father. Add photographs.

Name _____

Appearance _____

Age _____

Nationality _____

Personaity _____

Life story _____

_____

Youth _____

Education _____

Profession or trade _____

Married Life _____

Children _____

Interests _____

Contributions to the family _____

_____

Your relationship to him _____

How were you similar to him? _____

How were you different from him? _____

If he left the country where he was born, explain the reasons and other facts about him place of origin.

_____

Title_____

Theme _____

Family

Brother

Describe your brother. Add photographs.

Name _____

Appearance _____

Age _____

Nationality _____

Personaity _____

Life story _____

_____

Youth _____

_____

Education _____

Profession or trade _____

Married Life _____

Children _____

Interests _____

Contributions to the family _____

_____

Your relationship to him _____

How did you feel about him then and now? _____

How were you different from him? _____

Other facts about his life _____

Title _____

Theme _____

Family

Sister

Describe your sister. Add photographs.

Name _____

Appearance _____

Age _____

Nationality _____

Personaity _____

Life story _____

_____

Youth _____

_____

Education _____

Profession or trade _____

Married Life _____

Children _____

Interests _____

Contributions to the family _____

_____

Your relationship to her _____

How did you feel about her then and now? _____

_____

How were you different from her?

Other facts about her life _____

Title _____

Theme _____

NOTES

Life Story

Youth

Earliest Memory

What is your earliest memory? Tell about one memory.

_____
_____
_____
_____
_____
_____
_____
_____
_____
_____
_____
_____
_____
_____
_____
_____

Title _____
Theme _____

Parents

Mother

Who was your mother? (natural, adopted) _____

_____

Describe her _____

_____

What were her assets? _____

What were her faults? _____

How was your relationship with her? _____

_____

Did she stay home or work outside the home? _____

Father

Who was your father? _____

Describe him _____

What was his job or profession? _____

What were his assets? _____

What were his faults? _____

How was your relationship? _____

_____

What memories do you have of your parents together? _____

_____

_____

How did you feel about your parents? _____

_____

Title _____

Theme _____

Family Life

What were the happiest memories of life in your family?

_____
_____
_____
_____

How did you know that your parents were happy or unhappy?

_____
_____
_____
_____

What happy times did you share with your parents and family? (Travel, sports, musical experiences, music, art, games, holidays and sharing chores.) Add photographs.

_____
_____
_____
_____

What sad times did your family experience?

_____
_____
_____
_____

Siblings

Who were your brothers?

_____
_____
_____
_____

Sisters?

_____
_____
_____
_____

What are your fondest memories of them?

_____
_____
_____
_____

What was your relationship with them? Then and now?

_____
_____
_____
_____

Title _____

Theme _____

Appearance

What did you look like? Add photographs.

Size _____

Hair _____

Skin _____

Eyes _____

_____

How have your looks changed?

_____

_____

_____

What physical or emotional problems did you have that affected your appearance?

_____

_____

_____

What part of your body caused you problems? (Height, hair or skin color, weight, nose size or complexion)

_____

_____

_____

Title _____

Theme _____

Religion

Did you grow up in a religious family? _____
_____

What was your religion? _____
_____

Where do you attend religious services? _____
_____

Explain the services. _____
_____

How were you affected by this training? _____
_____
_____

What character and personality traits were formed by your religious training? _____
_____

Did you ever want to pursue a religious vocation? _____

What memories do you have of your religious rituals? _____
_____

Baptism _____
Marriage _____
Death _____
Other _____
How did you perceive spirituality? _____
How did you feel about your religious training? _____
Title _____
Theme _____

Holidays

What holiday traditions do you remember?

Religious holidays _____

_____

_____

St. Patrick's Day _____

_____

Mother's Day _____

_____

Father's Day _____

_____

Memorial Day _____

Fourth of July _____

Labor Day _____

Birthdays _____

_____

Columbus Day _____

Martin Luther King, Jr. Day _____

Valentine's Day _____

_____

Thanksgiving _____

_____

Add other holidays celebrated in your country or province. How did you feel about them? _____

Title_____

Theme _____

Foods And Beverages

What food and beverages were popular in your family and in the culture? (Hot dogs - America)

_____
_____
_____
_____

How were specialty foods part of your family traditions or holidays?

_____
_____
_____
_____

Was dining with the family a tradition? Did you continue these traditions? _____

_____
_____
_____

What role did music play in your celebrations?

_____
_____
_____
_____

Add your mother's favorite recipes in her handwriting. (Special pie or cake) _____

_____
_____
_____
_____
_____
_____
_____
_____
_____
_____
_____
_____
_____
_____
_____
_____
_____
_____
_____
_____
_____

Title _____
Theme _____

Economics

How did your parents make a living?

Mother _____

Father _____

What role did financial problems or affluence play in your youth?

_____

_____

If you lived during the Great Depression, what do you remember about the effect on your family life? Research the time to help you recall history.

_____

_____

How did the economics of your family life affect your money values and behavior?

_____

_____

What jobs did you have during your youth? (Family chores, selling lemonade, baby sitting, washing cars, or mowing lawns)

_____

_____

_____

How did you feel about these jobs?

_____

_____

Title _____

Theme _____

Emotional Intelligence

Were you learning skills and improving your emotional intelligence? How did others perceive you? _____
_____
_____

Did you exhibit any of these characteristics:

Awareness of self _____
_____

Impulse control _____
_____

Persistence _____
_____

Zeal _____
_____

Self-motivation _____
_____

Empathy _____
_____

Social deftness _____
_____

Self-control _____
_____

How did you feel about these qualities then? _____
_____

Title _____

Theme _____

Intelligence

Did you begin to show below, above or average intelligence? How did your parents perceive you? _____

Were you gifted? Which areas? _____

_____

_____

How did these strengths affect your life? Give examples. _____

_____

_____

_____

Did you enjoy school, reading and learning? _____

_____

_____

Were you inquisitive? _____

_____

_____

Did you have a learning disability? How did you overcome it?

_____

_____

How did you feel about your intelligence level?

_____

_____

What was you I.Q.? _____

Title _____

Theme _____

Education

Describe your educational experience.

	PreSchool	Elementary	Junior High
School			
Address			
Years Attended			
Grades			
Teachers			
Education (Subjects)			
Grades (Marks)			
Experiences (Social)			
Transportation to school			
Behavior			
Feelings			

Title _____

Theme _____

Homes

What town, state and country did you live in when you were growing up? _____
_____
_____
_____
_____

Describe your home, apartment, farm, cabin or ranch. Add photographs. _____
_____
_____
_____
_____
_____
_____
_____

What were your earliest memories of your home(s)?
_____
_____
_____
_____
_____

How was your home important to your family life? _____
_____
_____
_____

Describe your room--did you share it? _____
_____
_____
_____
_____

Describe the surrounding towns, cities or environment. _____
_____
_____
_____
_____
_____
_____

How did these surroundings affect your life? _____
_____
_____
_____
_____
_____
_____

Describe your feelings about your homes. _____
_____
_____
_____
_____
_____

Title _____

Theme _____

Friends

If you were the only child, friends played a big role in your youth.
_____
_____
_____
_____

Were you too shy to make friends?
_____
_____
_____

Who were your best friends?
_____
_____
_____
_____

Were you comfortable in social situations? _____

What recreational activities did you enjoy with them? (Hopscotch, board games, computer games, movies or talking on the phone)
_____
_____
_____

Title _____
Theme _____

Health

How was your health in your youth?
_____
_____
_____
_____

What childhood diseases did you contract? (Measles, chicken pox, diphtheria, other) _____
_____
_____
_____

Did you have a disability? _____
_____
How did you react to it? _____
_____

How was your emotional health? Were you stable or unstable? (Temper, depression) _____
_____
_____
_____

How did your health affect your life? _____
How was your attitude towards your health and life? _____
_____
_____

Title _____
Theme _____

Toys

What were your favorite toys? (Rocking horse, puzzles, bicycle, trains or board games) _____
_____
_____
_____

Which solitary games did you play? (Puzzles, playing piano, computer, reading, drawing, writing, television)_____
_____
_____
_____

What did you enjoy playing with your brothers and sisters? Friends?
_____
_____
_____
_____

How did you feel about your toys?
_____
_____
_____

Did you create toys and games? Describe them.
_____
_____
_____

Title _____

Theme _____

Sports

What sports did you enjoy?

Individual _____

_____

_____

Team _____

_____

_____

Which sports were you skilled in?

_____

_____

_____

_____

Which sports did you continue in your adult life? Why? Why not?

_____

_____

_____

How did you feel about physical activity and sports?

_____

_____

_____

_____

Has your attitude changed? _____

_____

Title _____

Theme _____

Recreation

Did your family include you in any recreational or sports activities: golf, fishing, boating, tennis, horseback riding, chess or travel?

_____
_____
_____
_____
_____

Did you take lessons? Where? At what age?

_____
_____
_____
_____
_____

Have you continued this hobby today?

_____
_____
_____
_____
_____

How did you fell about recreational activities?

_____
_____

Title _____

Theme _____

Vacations

Where did you vacation? (Beach, cruises, car trips)

_____
_____
_____
_____
_____

When? _____

Describe the most memorable vacation. Add photographs.

Where? _____

When? _____

Who was there? _____

What did you do? _____

_____
_____
_____

Why was it memorable? _____

_____

Have you returned there? _____

How do you feel about vacations?

_____
_____
_____
_____

Title_____

Theme _____

Music And Dance

Were you innately musical? Did you study voice, piano, dance or an instrument?_____
_____
_____
_____

What role did they play in your youth?_____
_____
_____

Were your parents skilled musicians? (Piano)_____
_____
_____

Did you attend musical events? Where? When?
_____
_____
_____

Did you inherit perfect pitch or rhythm? _____
Did your family enjoy opera, symphony or ballet? _____
_____

How did this training enrich your life?_____
_____
_____

How did you feel about music and dance?_____
_____

Title_____

Theme _____

Skills

What skills emerged at this time? Interview your relatives or friends to discover how they perceived you.

Artistic _____

_____

Intellectual _____

_____

Manual _____

_____

Scientific _____

_____

Social _____

_____

Who helped you learn these skills? _____

_____

Did you enjoy art and music, or manual and mechanical activities? (Acting, painting, computers, playing the piano or basketball, reading, acting, writing, or fixing cars) _____

_____

_____

How did these innate skills and interests determine your career choice? _____

_____

Title _____

Theme _____

Personality

Why would you characterize yourself as an introvert or extrovert?
_____
_____

What kind of disposition do you have? Examples? (Kind, happy, or sullen) _____
_____

Do you perceive yourself as having a good sense of humor?
_____
_____

What are your strengths? Examples?
_____
_____
_____

What are your weaknesses? Examples?
_____
_____
_____

Did you acquire personality traits that your parents or siblings possessed? _____
_____
_____

How do you feel about yourself? Are you similar to or different from your youthful personality? _____

Title _____

Theme _____

Character

Your character was formed by your family values, religious and educational training, plus society's values.

How did your parents and family help formulate your sense of right and wrong? Other traits? Be Specific. _____
_____
_____
_____
_____
_____
_____

Which traits do you have and how do you perceive yourself?

Ambition _____
_____

Integrity _____
_____

Fortitude _____
_____

Courage _____
_____

Honesty _____
_____

Morality _____
Others _____
_____

How did your religious training form your character?

_____
_____
_____
_____

How did your school experiences contribute to your character development? _____
_____
_____
_____

How did society play a role in your character development?

_____
_____
_____
_____

What other factor contributed to your character? (Friends or contemporaries) _____
_____
_____
_____

Did you feel good about yourself?

_____
_____
_____
_____

Title _____

Theme _____

Pets

Are you a veterinarian?
_____

What role did pets play in your youth?
_____
_____
_____
_____

Did you have your own pet? Name? Add photographs.
_____
_____
_____
_____

What other pets did the family have? (Dogs, cats, horses, tropical fish, birds, etc.)
_____
_____
_____
_____

How did you feel about your pets?
_____
_____
_____

Title _____

Theme _____

Milestones

All milestones are memorable. Recall some in your youth. When did you first:

Walk _____

Talk _____

Creep _____

Ride a bicycle _____

Ski _____

Play tennis_____

Hit your first home run_____

Catch a fish_____

Have your first accident_____

Get your first spanking _____

Go to school _____

Go to the hospital_____

Make your first friend_____

Fall in love_____

Earn your first paycheck _____

Fail in school _____

Get rejected_____

Have your first fight _____

How did you feel about these milestones? Which was the most exciting? Why?_____

_____

Title_____

Theme _____

The Arts

Were you innately artistic?

_____
_____
_____
_____

Did you study sculpture or painting? Where?

_____
_____
_____

Did you visit art galleries? Where?

_____
_____
_____
_____

What role did art play in your family life?

_____
_____
_____
_____

Is art your profession? _____

Add pictures that you painted when you were young.

How did you feel about the arts?_____
_____

Title _____

Theme _____

Politics

Were any of your relatives politicians?
_____
_____

What political party did they vote for? Why?
_____
_____
_____

How did the country's political situation affect your youth? (Prohibition, The Great Depression, war time, peace, "60s") Research these years.
_____
_____
_____
_____

How did you feel about politics?
_____
_____
_____

What political leaders did you admire? Why?
_____
_____

What political leaders did you dislike? Why?
_____

Title _____

Theme _____

Happy Times

What were the happiest times? Explain who, what, where and when they happened. _____
_____
_____
_____
_____
_____
_____

Why were they happy? _____
_____
_____
_____
_____

Do you recall more happy than sad times? Why?
_____
_____
_____
_____
_____

How did you feel as a youth? Happy or sad? Why?
_____
_____
_____
_____

Title _____
Theme _____

Sad Times

What sad times do you recall? Explain who, what, when and where they took place. _____
_____
_____
_____
_____
_____
_____

Why were you sad? _____
_____
_____
_____
_____
_____
_____

Do you remember feeling sad as a youth? Why? (Health, family problems, financial worries) _____
_____
_____
_____
_____
_____
_____

Title _____
Theme _____

Feelings

What general impression do you have of your youth?
_____
_____
_____
_____

If you were adopted or grew up in another family, how did you fit in?
_____
_____
_____
_____

Why was your youth happy? (Family, laughter, love)
_____
_____
_____
_____

Why was it a sad time? (Sickness, death, divorce)
_____
_____
_____
_____

How did you feel about your parents? (Love, hate)
_____
_____
_____
_____

How did you feel about your place in the family?
_____
_____

Do you have latent resentment toward anyone/anything? (Too many family responsibilities, neglect, poverty or extreme affluence, poor self-image, physical, mental or other abuse, learning disabilities, emotional problems, war experiences, physical or mental disability or a personal tragedy)

_____
_____
_____
_____

How have you identified and resolved these youthful problems? (Therapy)

_____
_____
_____

How have unresolved youthful problems interfered with your adult choices? (Marriage partners, professional life, or friends)

_____
_____
_____
_____

Title _____

Theme _____

Future Plans

What future plans did you have? (Become a skating champion, football, soccer or baseball player, professional painter, musician or doctor) Where did these ideas originate? (Skill, family interest or peer pressure)

_____
_____
_____
_____
_____
_____
_____

How did they become a reality?

_____
_____
_____
_____
_____
_____

Why did you abandon your dreams?

_____
_____

Title _____
Theme _____

STAGES

	Teenage	Adult	Retirement
MEMORIES			
PARENTS			
SIBLINGS			

	Teenage	Adult	Retirement
MARRIED LIFE			
FAMILY LIFE			
CHILDREN			

STAGES

STAGES

	Teenage	Adult	Retirement
GRAND-CHILDREN			
APPEARANCE			
EMOTIONAL INTELLIGENCE			

STAGES

	Teenage	Adult	Retirement
ECONOMICS			
WORK EXPERIENCE			
HOMES			

STAGES

	Teenage	Adult	Retirement
INTELLIGENCE			
EDUCATION			

STAGES

	Teenage	Adult	Retirement
HEALTH			
SKILLS			
SPORTS			

STAGES

	Teenage	Adult	Retirement
HOBBIES			
FRIENDS			
SOCIAL ACTIVITIES			

STAGES

	Teenage	Adult	Retirement
PERSONALITY			
CHARACTER			
MUSIC AND DANCE			

STAGES

	Teenage	Adult	Retirement
THE ARTS			
FOOD AND BEVERAGE			
HOLIDAYS			

STAGES

	Teenage	Adult	Retirement
VACATIONS			
TRAVEL			
RELIGION			

STAGES

	Teenage	Adult	Retirement
PETS			
POLITICS			
MILESTONES			

STAGES

	Teenage	Adult	Retirement
PROBLEMS			
HAPPY TIMES			
SAD TIMES			

STAGES

	Teenage	Adult	Retirement
FEELINGS			
FUTURE PLANS			
OTHER IDEAS			

7

COMPARISON OF STAGES

The second organizational approach to writing your autobiography is to describe and compare the stages of your life using the topics in the charts that are on pages 98 to 110. That is, describe your earliest memories and compare them to the memories in the other stages of your life (Teenager, Adult and Retirement years). How are they the same? Different? Your story may be titled: "My Memories Are Happy."

The next story or topic on the chart will describe and compare your changes in attitudes and perceptions about your parents. "My Parents Were Right," might be the title of your narrative.

Story Number Three will be a description and changing perceptions of your siblings. Continue writing comparisons for all the other topics.

This is an unique tool for self-discovery and understanding the changes in your feelings, attitudes, perceptions of people and life, and your motivation and behavior.

Your perceptions of life have changed. This chart will help you clarify your thinking about these changes and why your ideas have changed.

Comparisons

A comparison narrative includes both similarities and differences. Write your comparisons; give them titles. The following questions are guidelines for the aspects of your life you are comparing, as you perceived them in your Youth, Teenage, Adult and Retirement years. Here are two examples: _____

Compare memories in all the stages of your life that you have experienced. How are they similar?
_____
_____

Different?
_____
_____

Number Two Comparison (See page 98)

Compare your parents.
How are your parents similar?
_____
_____

Different from you?
_____
_____

Compare your perceptions of them in different stages of your life.
_____
_____

Similar?
_____

Different?
_____

Title _____
Theme _____

18

Career

Our work environment was instrumental in shaping our lives. For example, if you were an educator, school has changed. Teachers, their pay, discipline, school buildings, educational philosophy, materials and technology, parent and student participation, values (respect, honesty), abuse and violence in schools are all different today.

Major changes have also taken place in health sciences, business, transportation, entertainment, government, the arts and all of society. Evaluate and trace the changes in your work life or write a book about your life as a country doctor or teacher, fire fighter, policeman, pilot, farmer or professional football player.

What was your trade, profession or business? _____
_____
_____
_____
_____

What training was necessary for your career? _____
_____
_____

Other occupations _____
_____
_____

Occupation

Job Title _____
Place of business _____
Years of service _____
Salary _____
Duties _____
Vacations _____
Changes in the company's philosophy:
_____
_____

Changes in job description (More or less responsibility)
_____
_____

Changes in moral values (Honesty, honor, integrity, respect)
_____
_____

What did you enjoy about the job? _____
_____
_____

Why were you successful or not successful? _____
_____

Where did you have problems? _____
What did you dislike about the job? _____
_____
_____

Where did you travel on business? _____
_____
_____

Why would you choose this work again? _____
_____
_____

How did your work contribute to your life style? _____
_____

Title_____
Theme _____

9

CULTURAL CHANGES

Historical and cultural changes are interdependent. Historical events often determine society's values and they change, sometimes radically. You may have lived in the 60s where radical changes were apparent in the United States.

Trace the cultural changes in your country and how these values affected your life style and family. Use all available research: people, newspapers, magazines, books, films and photographs. Every year on your birthday, copy the front page of your local newspaper. They will trace cultural values.

Be sure to add your personal feelings about these changes in cultural values. Add your humorous anecdotes to the narrative.

If you lived in another society, trace the cultural changes in that country.

The Arts

The arts reflect cultural values and changes. Is it your profession? Describe your job. (Sculpture, painting, crafts, or graphics)
_____
_____
_____

Is art your hobby?
_____
_____

How much training or education do you have?
_____
_____

Do you paint real or abstract pictures? Include photographs of your work. _____
_____
_____

Have you won awards?
_____
_____

Write a story about the changes in the arts in your lifetime. Add your feelings about art.
_____
_____
_____
_____
_____
_____
_____
_____
_____

Title _____
Theme_____

Architecture

Architectural styles reflect cultural changes. Have you enjoyed a career in architecture, engineering or housing construction?
_____
_____

How has your job changed throughout your life?
_____
_____

Did you follow trends in housing and commercial buildings? Discuss these trends. _____
_____

Who is, or was your favorite architect? Why?
_____
_____

Have you designed a home or building? Include the design. Add photographs.
_____
_____

How have furniture designs and materials changed?
_____
_____

How do you feel about these changes? _____
_____

What is your favorite building in the world? Why?
_____
_____

Write a story about these architectural changes.
_____
_____
_____
_____

Title _____
Theme _____

Economic

The changes in economy are reflected in society's values.
Are you an economist? _____
Did you study business? Where? When? _____
_____
Compare the value of money:

	Your Youth	Today
Cost of bread	_____	_____
Cost of a movie	_____	_____
Cost of a gallon of gas	_____	_____

What has happened to the value of a dollar?
_____
How did the Great Depression affect you and your family?
_____
_____

Have you ever lost your job? How did you deal with the problem?
_____

How has inflation affected you and your family? (Retirement)
_____
_____

Do you have money problems? (Excessive spending, gambling) How did you solve them?
_____
_____

Do you budget your funds? _____
Do you have a consistent investment habit?
_____

What is your attitude toward money? _____
_____

Write about how your money attitudes have changed in your lifetime. Add your feelings. _____
Title _____
Theme _____

Education

	Primary School	Middle School	High School	College
Name				
Years				
Location				
Building				
Discipline				
Grades				
Curriculum (courses)				
Values (honesty, respect)				
Religion				
Teachers				
Principal				
Transportation (bus, walk)				
Activities (sports, clubs)				
Classmates (friends)				

	Primary School	Middle School	High School	College
Social Relationships (popular, outcast)				
Learning problems (strengths, weaknesses, attitude)				
Personality (shy, assertive)				

Add photographs, awards, trophies, and report cards. How has education changed in your lifetime? Be specific, use your chart.

_____
_____
_____
_____

How did you feel about learning and school in general? Were you a scholar? Successful? Happy? Why?

_____
_____
_____

What is your most vivid memory of school?

_____
_____
_____

What was your worst experience in school?

_____
_____
_____

Who supported you emotionally and financially? _____
_____

How did your training, or lack of it, affect your life? _____
_____

What do you think of home schooling, alternative education?
_____

How would you change schools today? _____
_____
_____

Have you ever been a volunteer, member of the P.T.A. or school board? _____
_____

Did you pursue a career in education? What? Where? How are you influencing our education system? _____
_____
_____

Has your education ended? What skill have you learned since finishing your formal education?
_____
_____

What courses and skills do you plan to study in the future? (Computer, foreign language, opera, golf)
_____
_____

Write a story about your education, and how you feel about it.
_____
_____

Title _____
Theme _____

Entertainment

Entertainment reflects society's values. The world of entertainment includes: movies, television, Hi-fi player, VCR, CD player and computer games. Which ones have you owned?
_____
_____

Did you have a career in this field? What area? Explain changes in wages, and responsibilities.
_____
_____

Radio: What role did radio play in your life? (Youth, Adult)
_____
_____

Movies: Which ones were your favorites?
_____
_____

How were the themes different then?
_____
_____

Why did you enjoy them?
_____

Who were your favorite actors? Why?
_____

Were you an actor, or aspire to be one?
_____

Television: When did you first buy a television?
_____
_____

What was your favorite program? Why? _____
_____
_____

How has the content of programs changed? Better or worse?
_____
_____
_____

Hi-fi Player Remember your first player? _____
_____

What records did you play? _____
_____

VCR Do you own a VCR? _____
_____

CD Player Do you own one? _____
Computer Do you own one? _____
Computer games: Which games do you play?_____
_____

Reading, games, cards and conversation were once a form of entertainment. How much time did you spend doing these activities?
_____
_____
_____

How much time do you spend now? _____
_____

How do you feel about entertainment in your life? _____
_____

Write a narrative about the role entertainment has played in your life.
_____
_____
_____
_____
_____
_____
_____
_____

Title_____
Theme _____

Family Structure

The structure of the family and values have changed during your life. Society's expectations determined much of our behavior. Consider these questions:

What was the role of your mother? (Stayed at home or worked outside the home?) _____
_____

What was your father's role? _____
Were they happy within the framework of these expectations?
_____

What was your role in the family? _____
_____

Did you have rules to follow? How were you disciplined?
_____
_____

How has your parental role changed?
_____
_____

For the better, or worse?_____
How was family life different in your youth? (Time spent together in conversation, recreation and work)._____
_____
_____

Society's problems often touch our lives. (Instant gratification, violence, lack of respect, alcoholism, family abuse, gambling, drug abuse) How were you affected by any of these problems?
_____
_____
_____
_____

Write a story about life in your family (Youth and Adult). Include your feelings.
Title _____
Theme_____

Fashions

Fashion trends reflect society's values.
Did you work in the fashion industry?_____
Did you design and sew your own clothes? _____
_____
Use photographs, magazines and newspapers to follow the trends in your lifetime.

Ladies' Fashions
Clothing, fabrics _____
Hair styles_____
Shoe styles_____
Accessories (Hats, belts, gloves) _____
Men's Fashions (Suits, shoes, jackets, hair styles)
_____
_____

How did you dress for school, your job and church? _____
_____
How do students dress today?_____
_____
Which era was your favorite? Most comfortable?
_____
What is your favorite color?
_____
Do you use it in your home?
_____
Have you always been "in style"?
_____

Write a story about how fashion has influenced your life.
Title_____
Theme _____

Foods and Beverages

Food and beverage trends reflect society's values, also. There were major changes in the food and beverage industry during your lifetime.
Did you work in the industry? _____
What changes did you observe? _____
_____
Did you live on a farm, ranch or grow a garden?
_____
What foods were popular when you were young?
_____
How were they prepared? _____
_____
Are you eating them today? Why or why not? _____
_____
How are growing methods different? (Hydroponic)
_____
_____
How have the meat and poultry industries changed? (Methods of raising animals) _____
_____
Beverages are different. Coffee, tea and cola are decaffeinated. Trace your drinking habits. (Soft drinks and alcohol)_____
_____
What is your favorite beverage? _____
Write your narrative, include feelings.
_____
_____
_____
_____
_____
_____
Title _____
Theme_____

Health

Society's attitudes toward preserving one's health have changed. What did you do growing up that you now know was unhealthy? (Experienced too much stress, exess alcohol consumption, smoking, overwork, excess weight, lack of exercise, or poor eating habits)

_____
_____
_____

Did you take vitamins daily? _____
_____

Have you been vital and generally healthy? Why not? _____
_____

How would you change your health habits?_____
_____

How have you solved them?_____
_____

How do you feel about preventative medicine ideas? _____
_____

Name some things that you practice to reduce stress._____
_____

Write a story about how knowledge about health issues has improved your life style. What lessons do you want to share with your children that will help them stay healthier?

_____
_____
_____
_____

Title _____
Theme_____

Language

Language is a reflection of society's values. New words express contemporary feelings and actions. Many new idioms have evolved or phrases that cannot be translated word for word into another language.

What is your native language? _____

Were you an English teacher? _____

What idioms have evolved in your lifetime? _____
_____
_____

What words are used today that have evolved in your lifetime?
_____
_____
_____
_____

Every profession has a vocabulary: education, medicine, engineering, computers, etc. Explain words used in your work.
_____
_____
_____

The definition of words has changed, also. Explain and show examples.
_____
_____
_____
_____

Think about the role that language has played in your life. Add your feelings, also. Write a narrative or poem about the changes in our language. Add humor.
_____
_____
_____

Title _____
Theme _____

Literature

Literature reflects the changes in society's values.
Are you a writer? _____
What have you written? _____
How have your reading habits changed? _____
Do you read fiction or non-fiction? Why?
_____
_____

Who were your favorite authors? Why?
_____
_____

Follow this author's books and writing style.
_____
_____

Do you read magazines or newspapers on a daily basis? Which ones?
_____
_____

How has literature reflected different values. (Science fiction, spy stories, mystery, romance novels) _____
_____
_____

Add a Best Seller list to your narrative.
What kind of non-fiction do you enjoy? (Self-help, psychology, relationships, religion, travel, how to books, autobiography) Why?
_____
_____

What is your favorite fiction? (Mystery, novels or romance)
_____
_____

Write a narrative about your favorite author. Follow his or her values as reflected in the stories. Include your feelings about the author's writings.
Title _____
Theme _____

Medicine

There have been major changes in the health sciences. Hospital sizes, specialization, patient information, preventative care and health insurance. They also reflect society's values.
Were you involved in health care? _____
How have you been affected by the changes in health care?
Illnesses? Your job? _____
_____
_____

Self-help and support groups for many medical and social problems are available. Have you utilized any of these resources?
Where? _____
When? _____
How did you benefit from them?
_____

The attitude toward psychological help has changed, also. In general, it is no longer a stigma to seek out guidance for difficult emotional problems. How have you availed yourself of these services?
_____
What were the results?
_____
_____

Write a narrative about a mental or physical problem that modern medicine helped you to solve, or a story about changes in medicine. Add how you felt about it.
_____
_____
_____
_____
_____
_____
_____

Title _____
Theme _____

Music And Dance

Music and dance are different today, they reflect society's values. Which kinds of music do you enjoy? Who are your favorite musicians?

Classical _____
_____

Jazz _____
_____

Dixieland _____
_____

Blues _____
_____

New Wave _____
_____

Country Western _____
_____

Religious _____
_____

Rock and Roll _____
_____

Other Kinds _____

What is your favorite instrument? _____
Why? _____
What musical instrument did you study? _____
Where? _____
Are you a professional musician? _____
How did your job change during the years? _____
_____

What music did you play and dance to in your lifetime?

    40s _____
    50s _____
    60s _____
    70s _____
    80s _____
    90s _____

What are your favorite dances?
- **Ballroom** _____
- **Country Western** _____
- **Ballet** _____
- **Modern jazz** _____
- **Square Dance** _____
- **Folk** _____
- **Hustle** _____
- **Disco** _____
- **Charleston** _____
- **Other dances** _____

What were your favorite dances in the past? _____
_____
_____

Other kinds _____
_____

How do you feel about music and dance?
_____
_____
_____

Write a story about your role in the world of music and dance.
_____
_____
_____
_____
_____
_____
_____
_____
_____
_____
_____
_____
_____

Title _____
Theme _____

Politics

Politics reflect society's values.
Did you have a career in politics? _____
What political party do you belong to? Has it changed? Why?
_____
_____

Do you volunteer to help your political candidates win elections?
_____
_____

How has the political philosophy of your party changed throughout the years? _____
_____

Which leaders did you admire and follow? _____
_____

What contributions to society did your party make? Research the history of the party. _____
_____
_____
_____

Trace its growth or demise. _____
_____
_____

How do you change laws? (Voting and writing letters to political leaders and work for the party) _____
_____
_____
_____
_____

How are society's values reflected in politics? _____
_____

Write a story about your involvement in politics and how you feel about the government in general.
Title _____
Theme _____

Population

Immigrants from other countries change society. They bring values from their countries of origin and they become integrated into American culture. Has there been a population explosion in the country where you grew up? _____
Population at your birth. _____
Population today. _____
Trace these changes during your lifetime. (Research)
_____
_____
_____

How are today's immigrants different? Trace the changes in your community. What was the population distribution? _____
_____

What countries did your ancestors come from? _____
_____

What values did they bring with them and instill in the family? _____
_____

How did society's values change as a result of immigration politics? (Research population and immigration) _____
_____

Describe your friends when you were growing up. Were they all the same nationality, religion, race?
School mates _____
Work friends _____
Family friends _____
Social friends _____
How are your friends different today?
_____
_____

Write about your country's population and people in your life or tell about your family's nationality characteristics and the role they played in forming your character.
Title _____
Theme _____

Recreation

Society's values regarding leisure time are reflected in business practices and finances. Many European countries have mandatory vacation times; in America it varies. What is the policy in your business?
_____
_____

How many hours do you work a week? (If retired, how many did you work?) _____
How did that change during your life time? _____
_____

How did you spend your free time? (painting, cards, conversation, boating, photography, writing, gardening, fishing, hunting, riding, reading, listening to music, films, pets, collecting stamps or antiques, travel.) _____
_____

How have your interests changed throughout the years?
_____

Has your financial situation changed your leisure time activities? How? _____

Have any of your hobbies become a vocation? (Gardener - opened up a flower shop, or photographer turned professional)
_____

How do you share your hobbies with others? (Publish your poetry or books, dog show, etc.)
_____

How much time do you spend enjoying hobbies alone?
_____

With others?
_____

Write a narrative about a hobby and your leisure time throughout your lifetime. Add photographs, awards, newspaper articles, poetry, stories, etc.
Title _____
Theme _____

Transportation

How were you involved in the transportation business: trolleys, cars, planes, boats, trucks? _____
_____
_____

Did you invest in stocks in any car company? When? How much? Evaluate them. _____
_____

When did you first learn to drive a car, plane or boat?
_____
_____

What did your first car look like? Add a photographs of all of them.
_____
_____
_____

What experiences did you have? (Accident)
_____
_____
_____

Have you ever flown on a supersonic plane or ridden on a bullet train? Where? What were your experiences?
_____
_____
_____

Write a narrative aout your first car or any aspect of transportation. Add feelings, photos.
Title _____
Theme _____

Travel

Travel is another leisure time activity. It satisfies a secondary need for new experiences. Are you involved in the travel industry?
_____
_____

Is travel your hobby? Has it always been an interest? Why or why not? _____
_____
_____

How has transportation affected travel opportunities? _____
_____
_____

Where have you traveled? Cost? Itinerary? Add photographs, passport pages souvenirs and journal entries. Include all you major trips.
_____
_____
_____
_____
_____

How has travel changed in your lifetime? _____
_____
_____

How have your attitudes toward travel changed? _____
_____
_____

Write a narrative or poem about travel in your lifetime. Add details and feelings.
_____
_____
_____
_____

Title _____
Theme _____

Religion

There have been changes in most every religion because it reflects society's values.
If you practice a religion, which one is it?
_____

Explain changes in:
Place of worship_____
_____

Method of worship _____
_____

Religious leaders _____
_____

Philosophy of the religion _____
_____

Decorum of worshipers (Dress and behavior)_____
_____

What religion did your family (parents) practice?
_____

Did you study and become part of your religion?
_____

As a youth or an adult?
_____

Do you consider yourself a spiritual person?
_____

What are your beliefs?
_____
_____
_____

Did you work in a religious field?
_____

Write a story about the role that religion played in your life and how you feel about it.
Title_____
Theme _____

Social Issues

Our country has social problems that have reflected society's values. **Abortion, women's rights, civil rights, feminism, crime and violence, family abuse and recreational drug use** are some of these issues. Which of these issues have you believed in and worked for? Why?

_____
_____
_____
_____

Which social issues have affected you and your family life and society? How?

_____
_____
_____
_____

Were you always treated fairly at work? (Pay and respect) If not, how did you solve the problem?

_____
_____
_____
_____

Write a narrative about a social issue that you were involved in or believed in.

_____
_____
_____
_____

Title _____
Theme _____

Society's Values

Are you a nurse, teacher, secretary or did you marry young? Your career was determined by limitations placed on women in the fifties. This is a good example of how society has experienced changes in values and behavioral changes. They have influenced everyone's life in some way.

Clarify your values and trace them through your life. Your behavior has reflected your beliefs. Use the chart on the following page. Add the years that you experienced.

What do you believe in now? Explain the changes these beliefs have undergone in your lifetime. Why?

_____
_____
_____
_____
_____
_____
_____
_____
_____
_____
_____
_____
_____
_____
_____
_____
_____

Title _____
Theme _____

VALUES CHART

Now separate the values and how you perceived society during these times.

	After the Depression	Sixties	Nineties
Female Roles (work place, home, sports)			
Respect (authority, law, other people and things, religion, education)			
Dignity			
Honesty (personal, work place)			
Pride (personal, work)			
Materialism (acquisition of objects, money)			
Present vs. Future Orientation (instant gratification)			
Morality (good vs. bad)			

When did you rebel against society? What were the results?

_____
_____
_____
_____
_____
_____
_____

Did society's values make life better or worse for you? Why? Use examples in your lifetime.

_____
_____
_____
_____
_____
_____
_____

How do you feel about society's present values? How can you change them?

_____
_____
_____
_____
_____
_____
_____

Write a story about how society's values changed your life. Use examples; add your feelings.

_____
_____
_____
_____
_____

Title _____
Theme _____

Comparison Of Societies

Compare the society that you grew up in versus today's society. There are distinct differences in values.

How is it different? (Marriage and divorce, leisure time, inflation and values) _____
_____

How is it better now than when you were younger? (medicines, new technology) _____
_____

Why is it easier to live today?
_____
_____
_____
_____

How is it harder to live in today's world?
_____
_____
_____
_____

When were you happier? Why?
_____
_____
_____

What have you done to bring a balance of old and new values into your lifestyle? _____
_____
_____

Write a comparison story of the old versus new societies and how they have affected you and your family. Add your feelings.

Title _____

Theme _____

NOTES

10

HISTORICAL EVENTS

If you lived through the Great Depression, a civil conflict or a war, these events played a role in your family life and the shaping of your personality.

By tracing the history of your country, you can describe the role that you played in these events and how they affected you and your family's life style.

This organizational approach to writing your autobiography will necessitate research. Interview your family and friends, review newspapers, magazines, movies and books. Locate your old and new photographs plus souvenirs to help you refresh your memory and add them to the stories.

If you grew up in other countries, their historical events shaped your life style, also. Do similar research to refresh your memory.

Include your feelings about all these events. Mental pictures help you to describe people, places and things related to your life during those times. Give each narrative an appropriate title.

These questions will help you recall the events associated with history. Think about them before you write your narratives.

World War I

There are very few living survivors of this war. Are you one of them?
_____

What part did you and your parents or grandparents play in this conflict? _____
_____

What experiences did you have during this time in history?
_____
_____

How did they affect you? _____
_____

What effect did the war have on your family?
Structure_____
_____

Finances_____
_____

Home _____
_____

Lifestyle _____
_____

How did you feel about it then and now? _____
_____

Have you ever returned to the battlegrounds?_____
_____

Write a story about the war. Add memorabilia.

Title_____
Theme _____

Roaring Twenties

Did you live in this prosperous era? _____

Where? _____

What was your life style? _____

Family _____
_____

Friends _____
_____

Work _____
_____

Finances _____
_____

Recreation _____
_____

Home _____
_____

How did the 18th Amendment that outlawed alcohol affect your life style? Did you go to speak-easies, dance the Charleston or enjoy jazz? _____
_____
_____

How did the 19th Amendment, women's right to vote, affect your life style? _____
_____
_____
_____

Describe your Model T Ford. Add photographs
_____
_____
_____

Did you own appliances: electric washing machine, radio and telephone? _____
_____
_____

What fashion trends did you follow? (Flapper, bobbed hair, cloche hat) Include photographs.
_____
_____

Did you read contemporary authors: Ernest Hemingway, Sinclair Lewis, Carl Sandburg and F. Scott Fitzgerald?
_____
_____

What did you think of these authors? Has your opinion changed?
_____
_____

How do they compare to contemporary authors?
_____
_____

Add photographs and other souvenirs of that time.
Write a story about this time of your life. Add your feelings about the times.
_____
_____
_____
_____

Title _____
Theme _____

The Great Depression

Where were you when the stock market collapsed on October 29, 1929? _____
_____

Were you one of the 12 million Americans out of work in 1931?
_____

How were you and your family affected financially? _____
_____

Emotionally? _____
_____
_____

How did you make a living? _____
_____
_____

How did you survive the Great Depression? _____
_____
_____
_____

What are your most vivid memories of life in that time?
_____
_____

What personality traits do you have today that can be traced back to your need to survive that difficult time? _____
_____

Write a story abut the Great Depression and how you felt at that time.
Title _____
Theme _____

World War II

What part did you and your family and friends play in this conflict?
_____
_____
_____
_____

What experiences did you have? _____
_____
_____
_____
_____

How did they affect you? _____
_____
_____

What effect did the war have on your family:
Structure_____
_____

Finances_____
_____

Home _____
_____

Life style _____
_____

How did you feel about it then and now? _____
_____
_____

Have you ever returned to the battle grounds? _____
Write a story about your role in the war. Add memorabilia.
Title_____
Theme _____

149

Atomic Age

Do you remember when the first atomic bomb was dropped on Japan in 1945? _____
_____
_____
_____

Were you in Japan at the time?
_____
_____
_____
_____

Have you ever visited Hiroshima or Nagasaki, Japan?
_____
_____
_____
_____

What were your reactions to this event?
_____
_____
_____
_____

Write a story about the Atomic Age, how it changed foreign policy and affected your life style.
_____
_____
_____
_____
_____

Title _____
Theme _____

Korean War

What part did you and your family and friends play in this conflict? (1950)_____
_____
_____
_____

What experiences did you have? _____
_____
_____

How did they affect you? _____
_____
_____

What effect did the war have on your family:
Structure_____
_____

Finances_____
_____

Home _____
_____

Life style _____
_____

How did you feel about it then and now?
_____
_____
_____

Have you ever returned to the battle grounds?
_____
_____

Write a story about your role in the war. Add memorabilia.
Title_____
Theme _____

The Sixties

The greatest social changes since the 1920s took place in the 60s. How did feminism, legalized abortion, recreational drugs, civil rights, rock-and-roll music, divorce, environmental pollution and the sexual revolution affect your life?

_____
_____
_____
_____

Which changes played the biggest role in your life? Why?

_____
_____
_____
_____
_____
_____
_____
_____
_____

What were your feelings about these changes?

_____
_____
_____
_____
_____
_____
_____
_____

Title _____
Theme _____

Civil Rights

Civil Rights was the leading national issue in the early 1960s.
_____
_____
_____
_____

Were you involved in this movement? How?
_____
_____
_____
_____
_____
_____
_____
_____
_____

What were your feelings about the cause?
_____
_____
_____
_____
_____
_____
_____
_____
_____

Write a story about the Civil Rights cause and the part you played in it. Add newspaper articles.
Title _____
Theme _____

Space Age

In 1962, John Glenn, Jr. became the first American to orbit the earth.

Were you a part of the space program in any way?
_____
_____
_____
_____

How did you feel about landing on the moon and space travel?
_____
_____
_____
_____
_____
_____
_____

Add newspaper articles to this story. Use old newspapers. Write a story about the Space Age.
_____
_____
_____
_____
_____
_____
_____
_____
_____
_____
_____

Title _____
Theme _____

War In Vietnam

What part did you and your family and friends play in this conflict?
_____
_____
_____
_____

What experiences did you have? _____
_____
_____

How did they affect you? _____
_____
_____

What effect did the war have on your family:
Structure_____
_____

Finances_____
_____

Home _____
_____

Life style _____
_____

How did you feel about it then and now?
_____
_____

Have you ever returned to the battle grounds?
_____
_____

Write a story about your role in the war. Add memorabilia.
Title_____
Theme _____

Persian Gulf War

What part did you and your family and friends play in this conflict?
_____
_____
_____

What experiences did you have? _____
_____
_____

How did they affect you? _____
_____
_____

What effect did the war have on your family:
Structure_____
_____

Finances_____
_____

Home _____
_____

Life style _____
_____

How did you feel about it then and now?
_____
_____

Have you ever returned to the battle grounds?
_____
_____

Write a story about your role in the war. Add memorabilia.
Title_____
Theme _____

Other Countries

If you spent your life or part of your life growing up and living in foreign cultures, recall and research the country's historical events when you lived there. Then write your story about how these historical events affected your lifestyle and education. Add memorabilia. Include your feelings about life there.

_____
_____
_____
_____
_____
_____
_____
_____
_____
_____
_____
_____
_____
_____
_____
_____
_____
_____
_____
_____
_____
_____
_____
_____
_____
_____

Title _____
Theme _____

11

HOBBIES

What is your hobby? Do you collect miniature doll houses, build wooden bird houses, race horses or attend movies? Trace this avocation throughout your lifetime. Include photographs, souvenirs, awards and other information about the role that the hobby played in your life.

You can tell your life story by explaining the objects in your collection. Each one reflects the cultural values of the time you discovered it and when it was formed or made. The style in clothing, cars, homes, music and themes in movies, books, television and magazines also tell the story of society at that time.

Relate your life story to these objects, the time and where you found them. All the facts about the object (history, description and cost) will tell more about your interests and personality traits in that stage of your life.

It may have been discovered in your backyard (Indian artifact or rock) or in a foreign country. Describe its origin and the historical events of the time. Was it war or peacetime?

Add color photographs of the objects and do the necessary research to explain each one.

Collection

What do you collect? _____

    angels   antique cars   art objects
    baseball cards books   bottles
    dolls   elephants   toy soldiers
    figurines   gemstones   glasses (goblets)
    hats   horses   Indian artifacts
    magazines   model trains   miniature doll furniture
    rare coins   rocks   records, CDs, tapes
                                                          stamps

Describe your hobby.
_____
_____

How did you get interested in it? (Inherited a collection, profession)
_____
_____

When did you start the hobby?
_____
_____

How do you feel about it?
_____
_____
_____

Will you continue it?
_____
_____

Title _____
Theme _____

Items In Collection

Itemize and describe the objects in your collection.
Collection _____
Item Number One _____
What is it? _____
Where did you get it? Tell about the circumstances surrounding its acquisition. _____
_____

What is it used for? Represent?
_____
_____

Describe it.
_____
_____

When did you acquire it? _____
Who was with you? _____
What was happening in your life then? (Stage)
_____

How does it reflect society's values? (Fashion, architecture, transportation) _____
_____

Why did you choose it? _____
_____
How much did it cost? _____
Describe its history (Rock or artifact) and the history of the country of origin. _____
_____

Where do you keep it? (Cabinet) _____
Do you continue this interest? _____
Add a color photo or sketch of each item in the collection.
Title _____
Theme _____

12

HOMES

The home is the focal point of one's existence - a place where basic needs are met and a center for learning and religious and moral training. Most people live in many places and in many homes during a lifetime. You can tell your life story by describing these experiences and feelings about each homestead.

Life on a sheep farm or cabin in the woods would be different from a beach house on the ocean or lake or an inner city housing project. Where did you live? Include information about the villages, towns or cities that you resided in. Research the location, climate, people, economy and politics; they are also important for understanding how your environment affected your lifestyle. Add photos of your house or apartment and a map of its location.

Then tell about the states and country - its history and politics. Were you living there during the Great Depression, World War II or the Civil Rights Movement? Research both the place and its history and culture.

Maybe you studied abroad or your father was in the military. Explain their cultures and how their values affected your education and development. Do additional research to enhance your memories of the culture.

Homes In Your Country

Name of house _____
Address _____
_____
Years you lived there _____
Members of family residing there. (Add photos)
_____
_____

Describe the exterior.
_____
_____

Describe the interior.
_____
_____

Describe your room.
_____
_____

Describe your favorite room. Why?
_____
_____

What were your fondest memories? (Celebrations)
_____
_____

What was the proximity to neighbors, friends, school, shopping, library and recreation areas?
_____
_____
_____
_____

How did the climate affect your home and life style?
_____
_____

Describe the town, city or village it was located in (Appearance, facilities).
_____
_____
_____
_____

Describe the state or province it was located in.
_____
_____
_____
_____

Describe the country that it was located in. (Economy, events that were shaping its history, people, language and culture)
_____
_____
_____
_____

What were your feelings about this home?
_____
_____

Why did you move?
_____
_____

Have you returned there? What did you find?
_____
_____

Title _____
Theme _____

Homes In Foreign Countries

Name of house _____

Address _____

_____

_____

Country _____

Years you live there _____

Family members residing with you

_____

_____

Appearance (Exterior)

_____

_____

Appearance (Interior)

_____

_____

Describe your room

_____

_____

What was your favorite room? Why?

_____

_____

What was your fondest memory?

_____

_____

_____

_____

What was the proximity to neighbors, friends, school, shopping, library and recreation?
_____
_____

How did the climate affect your home and life style?
_____
_____

Describe the town, city or village it was located near.
_____
_____

Describe the province it was located in.
_____
_____

Describe the country that it was located in. (Economy, historic events, people, language and culture)
_____
_____
_____

What were your feelings about this home and place?
_____
_____

Why did you move?
_____
_____

Have you returned there? What did you find?
_____
_____

Title _____
Theme _____

NOTES

13

HUMOR

Are you a gifted humorist, stand-up comedian or skilled at reparteé? Do you see the fun in life? Recall and collect examples of humorous incidents and include them in your book or write your life story using these comical experiences. Add cartoons, poetry, comic strips, anecdotes and jokes.

Describe or act out funny experiences, tell jokes, read comical stories for a more humorous auto-video tape. Write a script, wear costumes and use props or other visual aids.

_____
_____
_____
_____
_____
_____
_____
_____
_____
_____
_____
_____
_____
_____
_____
_____

Favorite Humorists

Who are your favorite humorists?
_____
_____
_____
_____
_____

Literature (Prose and verse)
Ogden Nash _____
_____

James Thurber _____
_____

Mark Twain _____
_____

Oscar Wilde_____
_____

Art Buchwald _____
_____

Stand up Comics _____
_____
_____

Movies and Movie Stars_____
_____
_____
_____
_____

Cartoonists (Political and Social) _____
_____
_____

Television Personalities _____
_____
_____
_____
_____

Others _____
_____
_____

What is your favorite comedy routine? _____
_____
_____
_____
_____

Humor can be silly or intellectual, sarcastic or satirical. Which do you enjoy most? Why? _____
_____
_____

How would your humor be described? _____
_____
_____

Do you use sarcasm? _____
_____
_____

How has it affected others? _____
_____
_____
_____

Kinds Of Humor

Recall and collect examples of humor that you created and enjoyed in your lifetime. Research them in movies, books, art, drama, music, comics and cartoons.

Situational Humor. The unexpected happening or when two unrelated things happen simultaneously.
_____
_____

Humorous Words. They often sound funny when pronounced incorrectly.
_____
_____

Hyperbole. A figure of speech, an exaggeration.
_____
_____

Puns. A play on words with similar sounds and double meanings. (This is an ancient form of humor which can be traced back to the ancient Greeks and Romans.)
_____
_____

Repetition. Repetition two times, then a third time it happens differently.
_____
_____

Parody. Change or rearrange words of a story for humorous effect.
_____
_____

Burlesque. Ridicule. (Gilbert and Sullivan sometimes poked fun at foods and cultural values.)
_____
_____

Slapstick. Crude and violent comedy or horseplay.
_____
_____

Farce. Exaggerated, ridiculous comedy used to fill in between acts in early theatrical performances.
_____
_____

Mimicry. Imitation of another person's speech or habits.
_____
_____

Reparteé. Quick, witty replies.
_____
_____

Irony. Understatement expressed by tone of voice.
_____
_____

Sarcasm. Hurtful humor.
_____
_____

Satire. Utilizes sarcasm and irony to expose human vices or political misdeeds. (Read *Gulliver's Travels* by J. Swift.)
_____
_____

Have you used your humor to heal an illness?
_____
_____
_____
_____

Research the physiological and psychological effects of laughter.
_____
_____
_____
_____
_____

Title _____
Theme _____

Humorous Experiences

Write about humorous experiences in your life.

Describe the incident.
_____
_____
_____
_____

When did it happen?
_____
_____

How did it happen?
_____
_____

Who was there?
_____
_____

Why did it happen?
_____
_____

Where did it happen?
_____
_____

How did you feel?
_____
_____

Title _____
Theme _____

14

JOURNAL

When I was a young girl, I owned a diary with a lock and key. It was my best friend - one who always listened and never judged. Writing in it made me feel better, but I didn't know why.

The diary is gone, but now I know the answer. There is valid research that encourages writing daily, especially about traumatic experiences. It helps you to clarify your emotional reactions and come to a resolution while improving your health and immunity by increasing T-cells (T-cells fight infections).

Recording your bodily reactions to people and events will give you valuable insights into stress-inducing situations. Notice if a person or event gives you a headache or pain in the neck. You can learn to interpret your body's reactions to people and other stressors and learn better coping skills. Add this to your entry.

Another advantage to writing daily is for future reference. If you are trying to make an important decision, daily data is good feedback for validating your behavior at a future time. It is written evidence of your personal feelings and helps clarify your thinking and motivate behavior.

If you still have your diary, reproduce it or detach the pages and add them to your book. Include your poetry and all the journal pages you have written.

Describe your emotions: sadness, loneliness, anger, fear, love or desperation. Be honest. Add these feelings to your daily journal entries.

Writing in your journal will become a habit. You'll find yourself reaching for a pen when you experience stressful situations.

Design a cover for your journal.

Journal Entry

Date _____

Place _____

Daily events in chronological order.

_____
_____
_____
_____
_____
_____
_____

Feelings and physical reactions to these events.

_____
_____
_____
_____
_____
_____
_____

Evaluate the day. How could it have been more rewarding?

_____
_____
_____
_____
_____
_____
_____

NOTES

15

LETTERS

Are you an avid letter writer? These topics and questions will help you recall and share your innermost thoughts and feelings. Give them serious thought before you begin. Write to anyone living or deceased who would enjoy and benefit from your ideas.

If you have saved letters from family and friends, add them to the book. Decorate borders with flowers or abstract designs, add color, cartoons and photographs. Use aboriginal designs on the border when decorating a travel letter about Australia. Add humor and poetry, too. Make each letter unique.

It should sound like you are talking to the person. Read them aloud while you record them. Then edit. Write all or some of the letters in your own handwriting. This personalizes them.

Add your own creative ideas. Don't be afraid to share your feelings about your life. Be honest. It will be cathartic and a good learning experience for both of you.

After the letters are completed, copy them for this book and mail some or all of them. Then add your responses. Choose appropriate, concise titles. The concepts in this chapter can also be incorporated into other parts of your book.

Natural Abilities

Think about your natural abilities. How did you use or misuse them?
What are your mental skills? _____
_____
_____

What are your physical skills? _____
_____
_____

What are your mechanical skills? _____
_____
_____

What are social skills? _____
_____

Are you gifted emotionally? What is your emotional intelligence? Evaluate how you and others see your behavior. Use personal examples.
Empathy _____
Self-awareness_____
Impulse control_____
Persistence_____
Zeal _____
Social deftness_____
Self-motivation _____
Self-control _____
How did it enhance or detract from your life?_____
_____

Which skills helped you make your living? How?
_____
_____
_____

Comparison With Parents

How are you alike and different from your parents?

Similar to Mother

_____
_____
_____
_____
_____
_____

Similar to Father

_____
_____
_____
_____
_____
_____

Different from Mother

_____
_____
_____
_____
_____
_____

Different from Father

_____
_____
_____
_____
_____
_____

Comparison With Siblings

How are you like your brothers and sisters? (Appearance, interests, personality)

Brothers
_____
_____
_____
_____
_____
_____

Sisters
_____
_____
_____
_____
_____
_____

How are you different from your brothers and sisters?
Brothers
_____
_____
_____
_____
_____

Sisters
_____
_____
_____
_____
_____
_____

Comparison With Children

How are your children like and different from you? Include size, personality, character traits, strengths, weaknesses, motivation and achievements.

Similarities

Daughters

_____
_____
_____
_____
_____

Sons

_____
_____
_____
_____
_____

Differences

Daughters

_____
_____
_____
_____
_____

Sons

_____
_____
_____
_____
_____

My Best Decision

What was the best decision you have ever made?
_____

When did you make it?
_____

What motivated you to make it?
_____
_____

What were the consequences?
_____
_____

Who was involved in it?
_____
_____
_____

Would you make it again? Why? Why not?
_____
_____

How do you feel about it now?
_____
_____
_____

Why was it your best decision?
_____
_____
_____
_____

My Worst Decision

What was the worst decision you ever made in your life? Include the circumstances surrounding it: time, place and people.

_____
_____
_____
_____

What motivated you to make this choice?

_____
_____

What were the consequences?

_____
_____

When did you make it?

_____
_____

Who was involved?

_____
_____

Why was it your worst decision?

_____
_____
_____

How do you feel about it now?

_____
_____
_____
_____

I Wish That I Had . . .

Finish this sentence: I wish that I had . . .

Most Exciting Experience

What was the most exciting experience of your life?
_____
_____
_____
_____
_____

When did it happen?
_____
_____
_____

Who was there?
_____
_____

What happened?
_____
_____
_____

Where did it happen?
_____
_____

How do you feel?
_____
_____
_____
_____

Most Frightening Experience

What was the most frightening experience of your life?
___
___
___

When and where did it happen?
___
___

Why did it scare you?
___
___

Who was there?
___
___

How did it happen?
___
___

Could it have been prevented?
___
___

How did it affect your life?
___
___

How do you feel about it now?
___
___
___

Funniest Experience

What was the funniest experience of your life?
_____
_____
_____

Why was it so humorous?
_____
_____
_____

Who was there?
_____
_____
_____

When and where did it happen?
_____
_____
_____

How did you feel?
_____
_____
_____

Add jokes, cartoons or other examples of your original humor.
_____
_____
_____
_____
_____

Best Learning Experience

What was your best learning experience?
_____
_____
_____

Who was there?
_____
_____
_____

What happened?
_____
_____
_____

Where did you experience it?
_____
_____
_____

When did it happen?
_____
_____
_____

How did you feel?
_____
_____
_____

Has it been repeated?
_____
_____
_____

Happiest Time

What was the happiest time in your life?
_____
_____
_____
_____
_____

Why was it so happy?
_____
_____
_____

Why did or didn't it continue?
_____
_____
_____

When did it occur?
_____
_____
_____

Who was with you?
_____
_____
_____

What are your memories?
_____
_____
_____
_____
_____

Saddest Time

What was the saddest time in your life?
_____
_____
_____
_____
_____

Why was it so sad?
_____
_____
_____
_____

When and how long did it take place?
_____
_____
_____
_____

Who was there with you?
_____
_____
_____
_____

What are your memories?
_____
_____
_____
_____
_____
_____

Best Day

When was the best day of your life? (Birth of a child, graduation)
_____
_____
_____

Where were you? (Describe the place.)
_____
_____
_____

What were you doing?
_____
_____
_____

Whom were you with?
_____
_____

Why was it the best day?
_____
_____
_____

How did you feel?
_____
_____

What are your memories?
_____
_____
_____
_____

Add photographs.

Worst Day

When was the worst day of your life? (Accident, death of a loved one or loss of job)
_____
_____
_____

Where were you? (Describe the place.)
_____
_____

What were you doing?
_____
_____
_____

Who was there?
_____
_____

Why was it the worst day?
_____
_____

How did you feel?
_____
_____

What are your memories?
_____
_____
_____
_____

Add photographs.

Favorite Hobbies

What hobbies have you enjoyed? (Collections, photography, reading, writing, chess, movies or poetry)

_____
_____
_____
_____
_____

Why?

_____
_____
_____

When?

_____
_____
_____

Explain them.

_____
_____
_____

How have they enriched your life? Emotionally? Financially?

_____
_____
_____

How did you feel about them?

_____
_____
_____
_____

Most Beautiful Sight

Describe the most beautiful sight that you have ever seen.
___
___
___
___
___

Where was it?
___
___
___
___

When did you see it?
___
___
___

Who was with you?
___
___
___

What did you see?
___
___
___
___

How did you feel?
___
___
___

Add a photograph of it.

Most Memorable Sight

Maybe you remember a sight that was sad or provoked strong feelings of anger, fear or sympathy. This makes it memorable.

Describe the sight.
_____
_____
_____
_____

When was it?
_____
_____
_____

Where was it?
_____
_____
_____

Who was there?
_____
_____
_____

What was happening?
_____
_____
_____

How did you feel?
_____
_____
_____

Have you ever seen it again? _____
_____

Friends At Different Stages

Who were your friends?

Youth
_____
_____

Teenage Years
_____
_____

Adult
_____
_____
_____

Retirement
_____
_____
_____

Why did you choose them?
_____
_____

Did they continue to be friends? Why? Why not?
_____
_____
_____

How do you feel about friends?
_____
_____
_____
_____

Most Influential Person

Who was the most influential person in your life?
_____
_____
_____

Why was this person influential?
_____
_____
_____

How did this person enrich your life?
Intellectually
_____
_____
_____

Emotionally
_____
_____
_____

Spiritually
_____
_____
_____

Explain why this person was so influential.
_____
_____

Have you been an influence on others?
_____
_____

Whom did you influence? Why?
_____
_____
_____

People I Have Admired

Name four people whom you have admired.
1 _____
2 _____
3 _____
4 _____

Why did you admire them?
_____
_____
_____
_____
_____

How did you admire them? (Votes, if politician, praise, etc.)
_____
_____
_____

Where did they live?
_____
_____

When did they live?
_____
_____

How did you feel about their lives and contributions to humanity?
_____
_____
_____
_____

How did they influence your thinking?
_____
_____
_____
_____

Difficult People In My Life

Who were the most difficult people in your life?
1 _____
2 _____
3 _____
4 _____

When did they live?
_____
_____
_____

Why were they difficult?
_____
_____
_____

Where were they?
_____
_____
_____

How did you feel about them?
_____
_____
_____

What did you learn from them?
_____
_____
_____
_____

How did their difficult behavior affect you?
_____
_____
_____
_____
_____

My Favorite Place

Where is your favorite place in the whole world?
_____
_____

When were you there?
_____
_____

Describe the weather, landscape, people, culture and other reasons for choosing it.
_____
_____
_____
_____
_____

Do you live there now or will you ever live there?
_____
_____

Why was it your favorite place?
_____
_____
_____

How did you find it?
_____
_____

Who was with you there?
_____

How did you feel there?
_____
_____

Add a photograph.

Philosophy Of Life

What do you believe in? List ten principles that you practice daily.

1 _____
2 _____
3 _____
4 _____
5 _____
6 _____
7 _____
8 _____
9 _____
10 _____

Why were they important in your life?

_____
_____
_____
_____
_____
_____
_____
_____
_____
_____
_____
_____

How did they evolve?

_____
_____
_____
_____
_____
_____
_____
_____
_____
_____

Best Advice

Your philosophy of life determines your behavior and the advice that you would give others. Using the ten principles, give advice. Include all your mistakes and successes.

_____
_____
_____
_____
_____
_____
_____
_____
_____
_____
_____
_____
_____
_____
_____
_____
_____
_____
_____
_____
_____
_____
_____
_____
_____
_____
_____
_____
_____

Apology Letter

Do you owe anyone (living or dead) an apology letter? Accepting responsibility for one's behavior is a sign of maturity. Think about the times you wronged this person, either on purpose or by mistake. Write more than one letter if you need to apologize to more than one person.

Whom did you wrong?
_____
_____
_____
_____

How?
_____
_____
_____
_____
_____
_____

What were the circumstances?
_____
_____
_____
_____
_____
_____

How did you feel about this wrong?
_____
_____
_____
_____
_____

Mail it if you feel that is appropriate.

Trips I Have Enjoyed

Describe five trips that you have enjoyed, when and where you went.

1 _____
_____
_____
_____

2 _____
_____
_____
_____

3 _____
_____
_____
_____

4 _____
_____
_____
_____

5 _____
_____
_____
_____

Why were they so memorable?
_____
_____
_____

How do you feel about them now?
_____
_____
_____

How I See Myself

How do you see yourself today? Who are you? What do you stand for?

_____
_____
_____
_____
_____
_____
_____

How have you changed or remained the same?

_____
_____
_____
_____
_____
_____

Do you like what you see? Why or why not?

_____
_____
_____
_____
_____
_____

What are you doing to change the things you don't like about yourself?

_____
_____
_____
_____
_____
_____
_____

How I Would Change Myself

What don't you like about yourself?

1 _____
  _____

2 _____
  _____

3 _____
  _____

4 _____
  _____

5 _____
  _____

What traits do you have that others don't like?
_____
_____

Why are these traits undesirable?
_____
_____

How do these traits make you feel?
_____
_____

How can you change them?
_____
_____
_____
_____

How I Would Change My Life

What would you like to be doing at this minute?
_____
_____
_____
_____
_____
_____

Where would you like to be?
_____
_____
_____
_____
_____
_____
_____

With whom? Would you rather be alone?
_____
_____
_____
_____
_____
_____
_____

After you have determined these changes, which ones are realistic and can be changed? Remember you must know your needs before you can change your life.
_____
_____
_____
_____
_____
_____

Plans To Change My Community

Do you believe that you can make a difference in your community by being involved in social issues: politics, domestic abuse, women's rights, environmental problems, or health and medical problems of the older population? Could you use your talents to work with disadvantaged children, sick and elderly or the literacy program?

What are you doing for the community?
_____
_____
_____
_____
_____
_____
_____

Where do you work?
_____
_____
_____
_____
_____

Whom do you work with?
_____
_____
_____
_____
_____

How does it make you feel?
_____
_____
_____
_____
_____

Plans To Change The World

Ask yourself: If I were in position to change the world, what would I change? Put yourself in the President's place, how would you use your influence to make global reforms. Poverty, hunger, poor housing and health conditions, exploitation of children, civil wars - the list is endless. What can you do within the framework of your community to make a contribution?

List two global problems most disturbing to you.
1 _____
2 _____

Why do they disturb you?
_____
_____
_____
_____
_____
_____
_____
_____
_____

How can you help? Political and religious groups are ideas to explore.
_____
_____
_____
_____
_____
_____
_____
_____
_____
_____

Contributions To Humanity

What are some of the ways that you will leave the world a better place? Are you using your talents to contribute to humanity? Consider your job, hobby or volunteer work. Did you write a book, build a house, write political legislation, invent a tool? Think about this and list your contributions.

What did you contribute to humanity? (Profession or volunteer work)
_____
_____
_____
_____
_____
_____
_____

When?
_____
_____
_____
_____
_____
_____
_____

Did you use your talents?
_____
_____
_____
_____
_____

How do you feel about these contributions?
_____
_____
_____
_____
_____
_____
_____

Plans For The Future

What do you intend to do in the future? List 5 goals.

1 _____

2 _____

3 _____

4 _____

5 _____

Why have you made these plans?
_____
_____
_____

Whom do they include?
_____
_____
_____

Where do they take place?
_____
_____
_____

How do you feel about them?
_____
_____
_____
_____

NOTES

16

Photography

Are you a collector of family photos or a photographer? You can use pictures as a theme for your autobiography.

Choose fifty of your favorite ones and write a narrative about each one. Select ones at different stages of your life: Birth, Youth, Teenage, Adult, Retirement.

Add photos of your travel and other experiences. If you need help explaining society at the time that it was taken, do additional research and interview people who were there or in the photo.

For example, you may choose one of you sitting on a pony. Title the story: "I Always Wanted a Horse." Then describe your lifelong interest in horses.

Add the picture to the narrative or mount it on the page to the left of the story. Frame it with your original design.

The placement of the picture will be determined by its size. You can mount it on the top, bottom or either side of the story. Be creative; make the page look attractive.

If you are a poet, add verse to your pictures and narratives. That tells a story, also.

Selection Of Photos

You can use both your own and other photos to tell your story of your life.

Select the very best pictures of yourself. Choose ones from all the stages of your life (Birth, Youth, Teenage Years, Adult life, Retirement). Write a narrative or poem about each one.

Choose fifty or more pictures. Add a title to each one. Enlarge or refinish them.

Add outstanding photos of countries that you have traveled to and tell about the culture of that place.

Write a title for each picture. It should be concise and reflect the mood. Keep them in chronological order.

1. Title _____
2. Title _____

3. Title _____
4. Title _____

5. Title _____
6. Title _____

7. Title _____
8. Title _____

9. Title _____
10. Title _____

11. Title _____
12. Title _____

13. Title _____
14. Title _____

15. Title _____
16. Title _____

17. Title _____
18. Title _____

19. Title _____
20. Title _____

21. Title _____
22. Title _____

23. Title _____
24. Title _____

25. Title _____
26. Title _____

27. Title _____
28. Title _____

29. Title _____
30. Title _____

31. Title _____
32. Title _____

33. Title _____
34. Title _____

35. Title _____
36. Title _____

37. Title _____

38. Title _____

39. Title _____
40. Title _____

41. Title _____
42. Title _____

43. Title _____
44. Title _____

45. Title _____
46. Title _____

47. Title _____
48. Title _____

49. Title _____
50. Title _____

Description

Describe each of the fifty photographs individually. Get help with the details from the photographer or people in them.

Photograph Number One _____
Who is in the picture?
_____
_____

When was it taken?
_____

Where were you?
_____

What was happening that day?
_____
_____

How did you feel at the time?
_____
_____

How does this photo reflect society's values? (Fashion, sports, transportation, architecture) Research additional information.
_____
_____

Where did the photo come from? (Parents' collection or your collection)
_____

Why did you choose this one?
_____

Other facts about the picture.
_____
_____

NOTES

17

POETRY

Poetry is a method for expressing sorrow at the death of a loved one or happiness at the birth of a child. Feelings can be shared in fewer words; it's a more concise way to share your feelings.

Tell your life story in free or rhyming verse. Write a few poems in your own handwriting and illustrate them with sketches, paintings, photographs or pictures from a magazine.

Write a poem like a narrative. Decide on a title and theme for each one. It needs focus also. Choose one topic and share your feelings about it. Add humor if it is appropriate.

Try writing free verse; it doesn't have to rhyme. If you don't write a book of poetry, then experiment with a few poems and add them to your book. Read some contemporary poetry for ideas or attend a workshop. It's never too late to explore new writing styles.

Write a short paragraph explaining the incident or experience at the beginning of the poem (top of the page or on the page to the left). The explanation is necessary to clarify the situation and your feelings.

Poems

Choose a funny or sad incident in your life and write a poem about it.
Theme: _____
_____
_____

Title: _____

Description of the background or what motivated you to write it:
_____
_____
_____
_____
_____
_____
_____
_____
_____
_____

Poem
_____
_____
_____
_____
_____
_____
_____
_____
_____
_____
_____

18

THEME

Were you persecuted and escaped to America? Did you fight in a resistance army or world war? Were you a country doctor or teacher? Explorer? Mountain climber? You can write a book about one subject or time in your life that elicited a strong emotional response: fear, love, anger, hatred.

If you experienced hardship or war or a sad or exciting time in your life, it would stand out in your memories. For, oftentimes, these traumatic experiences are never forgotten and affect us for many years, even a lifetime. Ask yourself this question: What was the most exciting or frightening part of my life? The answer can be the subject of a book.

Collect all memorabilia, research the time, and interview people who were with you to help you recall the experiences. Add photographs, poetry, letters, newspaper articles, magazines and direct quotes from others.

You can also write a travel book. Write narratives about either one memorable trip or all your travel experiences. Add photographs and impressions. Do research about the culture. Make your story interesting; add personal experiences. Give the book a simple title, work on a good lead, use vivid word pictures and conversation. Write in your own voice. Edit it very carefully. You might want to share your story with the world; if so, then find an agent and publisher.

You can either write the story as it happened, chronologically or begin in the middle of the story and go back to the beginning. Many experienced authors feel that the second approach is more difficult. Write a series of narratives and evaluate the results.

Refer to Part I of this book to refresh your basic writing skills. Use the ideas for writing and editing your book.

You can also weave your life story into a theme book or write your autobiography plus another theme book. Whichever method you choose, write a story that reflects your happiness, successes and your sorrows. Make it a candid story of your life, one to be shared that also offers pragmatic suggestions for living a happy life.

Locate contemporary, theme autobiographies. Why are they popular? Write their themes in one sentence.

Choosing A Theme

What was the most memorable phase of your life? Divorce, disability (mental, physical), survival of a natural disaster (hurricane), or plane crash, abuse, major illness, death of spouse or child, escape from a country, addiction, bringing up a family, story of your grandparents' trip to America or a sailing trip around America. If none of the above stands out as being important, then you may not want to take this approach to your book.

However, if there is a strong desire to write your story, answer these questions:

What was the experience? _____
_____
_____
_____
_____

Who was there? _____
_____

Where did it take place? _____
_____

When did it take place? _____
_____

How did you feel? _____
_____

Write the theme of the book. _____
_____

What is the title of the book? _____
_____

Chapters

Title the narratives or chapters in the book sequentially and add a theme for each one.

1 _____
_____
2 _____
_____
3 _____
_____
4 _____
_____
5 _____
_____
6 _____
_____
7 _____
_____
8 _____
_____
9 _____
_____
10 _____
_____

Write the story as you lived it. Add word pictures, conversation and suspense. Draft and edit carefully. Decide if you want to publish your story. Start by sharing it with a fellow writer. Then submit a chapter to an appropriate magazine. (See Publish, Part I)

Travel

You can write a travel book. Choose your favorite trip or many destinations and write travel stories. Include facts about the culture, people, geography, etc. Add photographs, souvenirs and pages from your expired passports. Give them a title and add your feelings about the destinations.

Destination _____
Title _____
Theme _____

Destination _____
Title _____
Theme _____

Destination _____
Title _____
Theme _____

Destination _____
Title _____
Theme _____

Destination _____
Title _____
Theme _____

Destination _____
Title _____
Theme _____

Destination _____
Title _____
Theme _____

Theme _____

Destinations

Destination number one.

Name _____

Location in world _____

Itinerary and map _____

Cultural information

    People _____
    History _____
    Climate _____
    Agriculture _____
    Economics _____
    Politics _____
    Social Problems _____
    Political Problems _____
    Foods and Beverages _____
    Education _____
    Recreation _____
    Tourist Attractions _____
    Arts _____
    Dance _____
    Manufacturing _____
    Government _____
    Chief Products _____
    Other Facts _____

Feelings about the destination

_____
_____

Title_____
Theme _____

19

ECLECTIC

You may elect to write your autobiography using all the ideas in Part II of this book: historic events, cultural changes, hobbies, journal, photography, poetry, letters, homes, theme approach, auto-video tape, chronological order, comparison of stages, and career. Then add photography, humor, poetry, letters, collections, journal entries, homes and compare stages to your story. Include three-dimensional objects in the Auto-Video Tapes.

These are only a few ideas. You can add others that interest you to your book. Be creative. There may be a topic that interests you that isn't included with these suggestions.

If you elect to incorporate all these ideas to create an eclectic book, it will be enjoyed by your family for many generations.

Organization Of Information

How do you plan to organize your information and materials?

1 _____

2 _____

3 _____

4 _____

5 _____

6 _____

7 _____

8 _____

9 _____

10 _____

What research do you expect to complete?
_____
_____

What are the three goals of this book?
_____
_____
_____

How does the eclectic approach satisfy your objectives?
_____
_____

Theme _____

Title of Book _____

20

AUTO-VIDEO TAPE

The last step in sharing your memoirs is to make a video tape. It adds another dimension to your story, a visual picture of you. Your voice, personality and appearance are another part of your being, different from your written story. Both the book and tape will be cherished by your children, grandchildren and friends.

Find a reputable videographer or ask a friend to tape your story. You will need a camcorder, the newest models have instant playback. Video your home, garden, car and surroundings. Participate in your favorite activities: cooking, painting, dancing, writing, playing the piano or reading. Add your friends and family to the video, and be yourself.

Include other videos: marriage receptions, religious ceremonies, retirement parties, graduation and trips that you have taken. They don't have to be professional. For you become both the star and director of this movie.

This chapter of the book suggests two ways to present your script. It has been organized chronologically, and the questions will help you tell your life story sequentially. Either answer the questions extemporaneously or read them. In both cases, you need an interviewer to ask the questions. Choose a family member to help with taping. A daughter and a son can interview their parents.

The second option is to use your favorite pictures for the themes in the video vignettes. They can be inserted on the screen as you talk or read your script. However, if you can't locate any photos, add other pictorial inserts and answer the book questions that will elicit information about your life.

Include documents (birth and marriage certificates, photographs), articles, poetry and other memorabilia for the video presentation. Now you can show three-dimensional objects. Use all the other organizational ideas in this book: family history chart, letters and essays about historical and cultural trends, journal entries, poetry, hobbies, collections, cartoons, and interviews with friends and family members, who were part of that time. Be creative for "This is Your Life."

When discussing the photo, ask yourself the usual questions: Who, What, When, How did you feel at the time? What were your mental images and feelings? Use this information to tell about each stage in your life.

The story begins with your grandparents and continues to the present (chronological order). If you have information about great grandparents, start you family history with them. Use as many photos as you have.

Research the historical times of both your life and all your relatives. It will help you to understand them. People tend to be good sources of facts about the Great Depression or the world wars. If you are talking about WW II, show your uniform and other memorabilia. Add letters from soldiers or letters that you wrote at that time. Your discharge papers can be inserted into the video, also. Show a map where you were stationed and add facts about your friends. Give information about the attitude toward the war. Add as much as you can remember to the pictures and the circumstances surrounding them.

If one stage or period in your life were exceptionally interesting or emotional, take more time to describe your feelings. You can write your script using this theme or read your book aloud. The topics for the stories have been narrowed down for you. Take the time to draft, revise and edit your scripts. Practice before taping.

Read your stories or talk extemporaneously, answering questions in the script as a member of your family interviews you. Tape in short segments of time. It will take two or three sessions to complete the project. Edit the tapes. You may want to add or delete information.

After you have completed taping, give copies to your favorite relatives and friends. Plan an Auto-Video Tape interesting to you, your audience and future generations.

GENEALOGY CHART

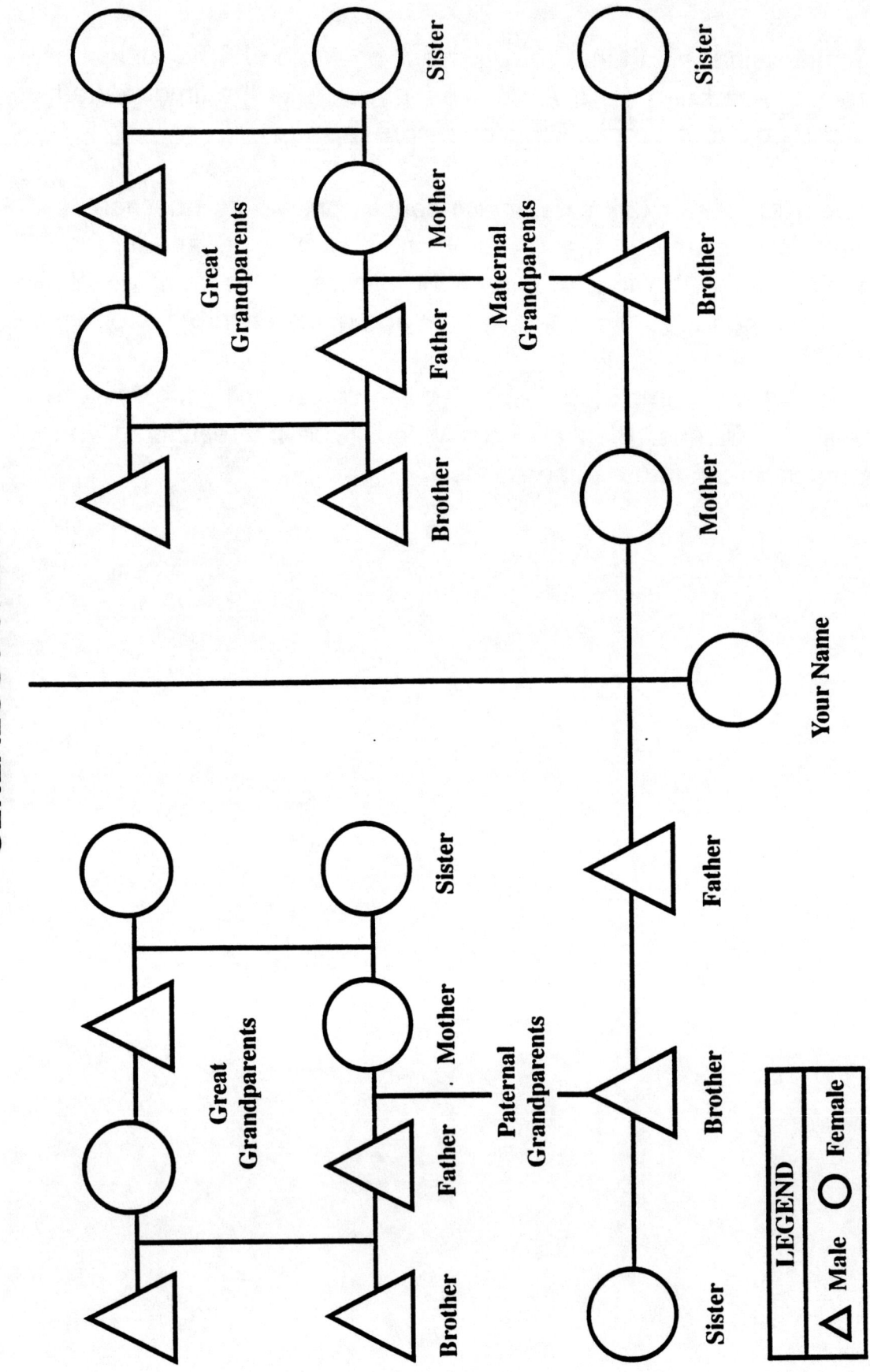

228

Grandparents

Maternal Grandmother

Grandmother on your mother's side of the family. If you don't have a photo of your grandmother alone, then use one of both your grandmother and grandfather and talk about both of them. If there is no picture, tell what you remember and have learned about her life.

Name _____
What is she doing?_____
Where is she? _____
With whom? _____
When was this picture taken? _____
Other things you see in it._____
Appearance _____
Age _____
Personality _____
Life Story _____
    Birth_____
    Date_____
    Place_____
    Youth_____
    Profession or trade _____
    Married life _____
    Children_____
    Interests _____
    Contributions to the family_____
    Death (Date) _____
    Place_____
    Causes _____
    Other facts_____
Script _____
_____
_____

Grandparents

Maternal Grandfather

Grandfather on your mother's side of the family. If you don't have a photo of your grandfather alone, then use one of both your grandmother and grandfather and talk about both of them. If there is no photo available, tell what you remember and have learned about his life.

Name _____
What is he doing? _____
Where is he? _____
With whom? _____
When was this picture taken? _____
Other things you see in it. _____
Appearance _____
Age _____
Personality _____
Life Story _____
    Birth _____
    Date _____
    Place _____
    Youth _____
    Profession or trade _____
    Married life _____
    Children _____
    Interests _____
    Contributions to the family _____
    Death (Date) _____
    Place _____
    Causes _____
    Other facts _____
Script _____
_____
_____

Grandparents

Paternal Grandmother

Grandmother on your father's side of the family. If you don't have a photo of your grandmother alone, then use one of both your grandmother and grandfather and talk about both of them. If there is no photo available, tell what you remember and have learned about her life.

Name _____
What is she doing? _____
Where is she? _____
With whom? _____
When was this picture taken? _____
Other things you see in it. _____
Appearance _____
Age _____
Personality _____
Life Story _____
    Birth _____
    Date _____
    Place _____
    Youth _____
    Profession or trade _____
    Married life _____
    Children _____
    Interests _____
    Contributions to the family _____
    Death (Date) _____
    Place _____
    Causes _____
    Other facts _____
Script _____
_____
_____

Grandparents

Paternal Grandfather

Grandfather on your father's side of the family. If you don't have a photo of your grandfather alone, then use one of both your grandmother and grandfather and talk about both of them. If there is no photo available, tell what you remember and have learned about his life.

Name _____
What is he doing? _____
Where is he? _____
With whom? _____
When was this picture taken? _____
Other things you see in it. _____
Appearance _____
Age _____
Personality _____
Life Story _____
    Birth _____
    Date _____
    Place _____
    Youth _____
    Profession or trade _____
    Married life _____
    Children _____
    Interests _____
    Contributions to the family _____
    Death (Date) _____
    Place _____
    Causes _____
    Other facts _____
Script _____
_____
_____

Family

Mother

If you don't have a photo of your mother alone, then describe the one you do have and your memories of her.

Name _____
What is she doing?_____
Where is she? _____
With whom? _____
When was this picture taken? _____
How she seems to feel _____
Other things you see in it _____
Appearance _____
Age _____
Nationality_____
Personality _____
Life story_____
    Youth_____
    _____
    Education _____
    Profession or trade _____
    Married life _____
    _____
    Children_____
    _____
    Interests _____
    Contributions to the family_____
    _____
    Your relationship to her_____
    _____
    Other facts_____
Script _____
_____
_____

Family

Father

If you don't have a photo of your father alone, then describe the one you do have and your memories of him.

Name _____
What is he doing? _____
Where is he? _____
With whom? _____
When was this picture taken? _____
How he seems to feel _____
Other things you see in it _____
Appearance _____
Age _____
Nationality _____
Personality _____
Life story _____
    Youth _____
    _____
    Education _____
    Profession or trade _____
    Married life _____
    _____
    Children _____
    _____
    Interests _____
    Contributions to the family _____
    _____
    Your relationship to him _____
    _____
    Other facts _____
Script _____
_____
_____

Family

Sister

If you don't have a photo of your sister alone, then describe the one you do have and your memories of her.

Name _____
What is she doing?_____
Where is she? _____
With whom? _____
When was this picture taken? _____
How she seems to feel_____
Other things you see in it _____
Appearance _____
Age _____
Nationality_____
Personality _____
Life story_____
    Youth_____
    _____
    Education _____
    Profession or trade _____
    Married life _____
    _____
    Children_____
    _____
    Interests _____
    Contributions to the family_____
    _____
    Your relationship to her_____
    _____
    Other facts_____
Script _____
_____
_____
_____

FAMILY

Brother

If you don't have a photo of your brother alone, then describe the one you do have and your memories of him.

Name _____
What is he doing? _____
Where is he? _____
With whom? _____
When was this picture taken? _____
How he seems to feel _____
Other things you see in it _____
Appearance _____
Age _____
Nationality _____
Personality _____
Life story _____
    Youth _____
    _____
    Education _____
    Profession or trade _____
    Married life _____
    _____
    Children _____
    _____
    Interests _____
    Contributions to the family _____
    _____
    Your relationship to him _____
    _____
    Other facts _____
Script _____
_____
_____
_____

Life Story

Birth

Locate photos and information about your birth. Show your birth certificate, the hospital, town and a picture. If you have a baby book, show the information in it.

Answer the following questions:
Name _____
Date of birth _____
Place _____
_____

Circumstances _____
_____

Parents _____
_____

Appearance _____
_____

What was happening in the country and the world? (Famine, depression, waratime) _____
_____

Other facts _____
_____
_____

Script _____
_____
_____
_____
_____
_____

Life Story

Childhood

Answer the following questions about this stage of your life. Add all the photos, documents, and memorabilia to enrich your story.

Explain your earliest memory. How did you feel? Who? What? When? Where? _____
_____
_____

How did your appearance change? _____
_____

Describe your home, town and country. _____
_____

Who were the members of your family unit? _____
_____

Who were your best friends? _____
What were your favorite toys and activities? _____
_____

What personality traits did you exhibit? _____
_____

What pets did you have? _____
What religious activities did you participate in? _____
_____

When did you crawl, walk, talk, read and write? _____
_____

What are your memories about school? (Grades, place, teachers, subjects and activities) _____
_____

What holidays do you remember? _____
What were your strengths and weaknesses? (Physical and mental)
What vacations were memorable? Where did you go and what did you do? _____
What were your feelings about the time? Why was it a happy or sad time? _____
Script _____

Life Story

Teenage Years

Answer the following questions about this stage of your life. Add all the photos, documents and memorabilia to enrich your presentation.

How did your appearance change? _____

_____

Describe your home, room, town and country. _____

_____

Who were the members of your family unit? _____

_____

Who were your best friends? _____

_____

What were your favorite sports? _____
Activities? _____
Clubs? _____
What personality traits did you exhibit? _____

_____

What character traits were you learning? _____

_____

What pets did you have? _____

_____

What religious activities did you participate in? _____

_____

What new skills did you learn? _____
What are your memories about school? (Grades, place, teachers, subjects, activities, etc.) _____

_____

What career were you working toward? _____
What holidays do you remember? _____

_____

Script _____

_____

_____

_____

Life Story

Education

Trace your education throughout your life and how it affected your financial status, sense of self-esteem and family life.

Education (School, degrees, training)
_____
_____
_____
_____

How it affected your finances.
_____
_____
_____
_____

How it affected your personality. (Self-esteem, skills)
_____
_____
_____
_____

How did it affect your family life?
_____
_____
_____
_____

How would you have changed your educational decisions?
_____
_____
_____

Script _____

Life Story

Early Adult Years
How did you spend your early adult years? (19-21) Military service, college, professional or technical training? _____
_____
Did you marry before you were 21? _____
When? _____
Spouse _____
Where did you meet? _____
_____
Children _____
Jobs _____
_____
Activities _____
_____
Homes _____
_____
Financial situation_____
_____
Religious holidays and activities_____
_____
Vacations _____
_____
Personality traits_____
Pets _____
Hobbies _____
Friends _____

What was happening in the country? _____
_____

What were your feelings about this stage? _____
_____
_____
Script _____

Life Story

Adult Life

How did you spend your adult years? Military service, college, professional or technical training? _____
_____

When did you marry? _____
Spouse _____
Where did you meet? _____
_____

Children _____
Jobs _____
_____

Activities _____
_____

Homes _____
_____

Financial situation _____
_____

Religious holidays and activities _____
_____

Vacations _____
_____

Personality traits _____
Pets _____
Hobbies _____
_____

Friends _____
_____

What was happening in the country? _____
_____

What were your feelings about this stage? _____
_____

Script _____

Life Story

Retirement

How did retirement change your life?
_____
_____

Where did you move? _____

Children _____

Grandchildren _____

Jobs or volunteer work? _____
_____

Activities _____
_____
_____

Financial situation _____

Religious holidays and activities _____

Vacations _____
Personality traits _____

Pets _____
Friends _____
Sports _____
Health _____
What were your feelings about this stage? _____
_____

Script _____
_____

Life Story

Evaluation Of Life

Think about your life and evaluate your decisions. Were you lucky? How?

_____
_____
_____
_____

How were you unlucky? (War, depression, health problems)

_____

How did you make important decisions? (Logic, emotion)

_____

What were your best decisions? (Marriage partner, education, occupation, financial)

_____
_____
_____

How did your initiative influence your life?

_____
_____

How did your faith, or lack of faith affect your personality in crisis situations?

_____
_____
_____

What are your feelings about your life?

_____
_____
_____
_____

Read some of your letters. (See **Letters**, Chapter 15)

Script _____

Life Story

Future Plans

How do you feel about the future? (Optimistic or pessimistic)
_____
_____
_____

What are your goals?
_____
_____
_____

Personal (Personality changes)
_____
_____
_____

Health (Exercise, weight loss)
_____
_____

Social (Friends, volunteering)
_____
_____

Financial (Investments)
_____
_____

Educational (Courses, travel, skills)
_____
_____

How are you implementing these goals?
_____
_____

Script _____
_____

NOTES

Bibliography

Berndes, Katherine R. *How to Write A Personal Narrative.* Gainesville: Displays for Schools, Inc., 1986.

Donnelly, Daniel A., and Murray, Edward J. "Cognitive and Emotional changes." *Journal of Social and Clinical Psychology 10 (1991)*: 334-335.

Goleman, Daniel. *Emotional Intelligence.* New York: Bantam Books, 1995.

Garvey, Mark, ed. *1996 Writer's Marker.* Cincinnati: Writer's Digest Books, 1995.

"Humor." *The World Book Encyclopedia.* 1994 ed.

Keene, Michael and Adams, Katherine. *The Easy Access Handbook.* Mountain View: Mayfield Publishing Co., 1996.

ADDITIONAL RESOURCES

Genealogy books available from
    R. Woods
    Consumer Information Center
    Pueblo, CO 81009

Using Records in the National Archives for Genealogical Research
Item #367A--50 cents
(Tells how to search for pertinent information: personnel, military and naturalization records, passenger arrivals, census reports and native Americans.)

Where to Write for Vital Records   Item # 145A--$2.25
(Provides name, address, phone numbers and instructions for ordering every local and state vital statistics office in the country.)

Appendix

TEENAGE
See page 98-110 for additional questions.

Memories - What memories do you have of your teenage years?
    What were your feelings then?

Parents - Who was your mother? Did she live at home?
    Describe her appearance and personality.
    What was your relationship with her?
    Did she work outside the home?
    Who was your father? Did he live at home?
    Describe his appearance and personality.
    What was your relationship with him?
    What are your memories of them?
    Were they happily married?
    How did you feel about them?

Siblings - Brothers and Sisters - Names and ages.
    Memories of them. Feelings about them.

Family Life - Were you happy in your family? Why? Why not?
    What activities did you share as a family?
    Was storytelling a family tradition?
    (Include your favorite story.)
    What prevented your family from being happy?

Appearance - What did you look like? Whom did you resemble?
    Were you over or under weight? Tall or short?
    How did your looks change? (Skin, hair, weight, height)
    What problems did you think you had?
    What parts of your body made you unhappy?
    (Nose size, hair color, height, weight, or a deformity)

Economics - How did your father or mother make a living?
    What role did money play in your adolescence?
    Were you a teenager during the Great Depression or a war?
    How did these events affect your family life?
    How did these events affect your attitudes toward money?
    How would you classify your family's finances? (Rich, poor)
    Did you work? Where? When? How much did you earn?
    What did you do? Explain your job.
    How did having money or lacking funds make you feel?

Homes - Where did you live when you were young? Farm, ranch, apartment?
    Describe your home: appearance, surroundings, your room.

What was the nearest town or village? Describe it.
What household chores were you assigned?
How did you feel about your home? (Too small, isolated, lonely)

Friends - Who were your friends? Did they live nearby?
What activities did you enjoy? (Sports, board games, music)
Have you remained friends with them?
How did you feel about friends? Or were you a loner?

Health - How did your health affect your teenage years?
Did it enable you to enjoy life? How? or Why not?
What diseases or sicknesses did you have? Problems?
How did you feel about your health?

Skills - What innate skills did you possess? (Intelligence, manual dexterity, artistic, musical)
What skills did you learn? (Piano, sports, typing, computer)
How did they affect your career choices?
How did you feel about these skills? (Appreciative, happy)

Recreation - What were your favorite activities? (Socializing, sports, talking on the phone, reading)
What were your favorite games? (Board games, cards)
What were your favorite quiet activities? (Reading, television, writing)
Did you enjoy club activities? (Newspaper, sport clubs)
How did you feel about recreation and having fun?

Sports - What sports did you enjoy? Why?
What teams did you play with?
Were you a good athlete?
How did you feel about sports?

Personality Traits - What traits did you possess? (Shy, extrovert, confident)
Has your personality remained the same?
What were your strengths? Weaknesses? Why?
Have they been resolved? How? Therapy?
Did you have a sense of humor? Has it changed? How?
How did you feel about your personality?
What was your activity level? (Active or quiet)

Character Traits - What traits did you possess? (Integrity, courage, honesty, perseverance, ambition, self-discipline and moral strength)
What traits did you lack? Why?
How did your family, religious training, education and society's values develop your character?
How did you feel about your character? Did you like yourself?

Intelligence - Did you perceive yourself as being intelligent?

How did you perform at school, home and socially?
What was your I.Q.? Did other people regard you as being smart?
How did you feel about your intelligence? Did you feel smart?

Emotional Intelligence - How was your emotional intelligence? (Self-awareness, impulse control, persistence, zeal, self-motivation, empathy, social deftness and self-control)
Did you have problems socially?
If you didn't have them, have you acquired these traits? (Therapy)

Education - Did you attend school? Where? When? Describe the teacher, classes, grades, extracurricular activities, your friends, favorite courses, memories, transportation, (bus, walk) the building, educational philosophy and your conduct.
What social skills did your acquire?
How did you feel about these years? How did they affect your personality?
How did these years affect your career decisions?
Answer the same questions about high school.

Religious Training - What was your religion? Is it the same today?
Did you attend church or services?
How did it affect your personality and character development?
Were you interested in a religious career? What religion?
How did you feel about the role religion played in your life?

Music and Dance - How was music a part of your life? Family life?
What instrument do you play? (Piano, organ, violin)
Do you have rhythm? (Innate or acquired)
Do you sing or dance? Attend theater, opera, ballet, the symphony?
Is music your chosen vocation? Future plans?
How did you feel about music and dance?

The Arts - Were you interested in fine arts? (Painting, drawing, sculpture)
Add photographs of your work.
Did you inherit these skills? From whom? Did you study painting?
Did you have an art studio in your home.? Who was the artist?
Did you visit art galleries and shows with your family and friends? Where, when? Who is your favorite artist? Why?
Was art your chosen vocation? What are your plans for the future?
How did you feel about the arts?

Vacations - What vacations do you remember? Describe place, people, time, and activities. Add photographs and souvenirs.
Did you ever attend summer camp? Where, when? With whom?
How did you feel about vacations? Today?

Foods and Beverages - What foods and beverages were popular in your home?

Who did the cooking? Was food valued?
Did the family dine together? Nightly or on holidays?
Explain your food preferences and traditions.
Add favorite family recipes.
How did you feel about food and eating?

Holidays - How did you spend holidays? What traditions did you follow?
Did all of the family share them? (Religious holidays, Fourth of July, Labor Day, birthdays, St. Patrick's Day, Columbus Day, Martin Luther King Day, Mother's Day, Valentine's Day, Thanksgiving, Father's Day, New Year's Eve, Memorial Day and other celebrations.)
What were your feelings about holidays? Did you enjoy them?

Pet - What pets did you have? Names? Kinds? Describe them.
Did you want to become a veterinarian?

Politics - Was there a politician in your family? (Dad, mother)
How did the country's political situation affect your teenage years?
How did you feel about politics? What party did you belong to?

History - How did the country's historical events affect your life? (The Great Depression, prohibition, war or peace, the 60s)
How did you feel about life in that era?

Milestones - What did you accomplish? (Drive a car, attend your first prom, have your first date, win your first prize, take your first plane ride)
When did you fail? Have your first fight?
How did you feel about your accomplishments?

Feelings - How did you feel about your teen-age years? Place in family?
Why was it a happy time? Sad time? Do you have residual anger?
What did you enjoy most? Least? How have these feelings affected your life?

Future Plans - What were your plans for the future? Educational goals?

ADULT
See page 98-110 for additional questions.

Memories - What are your fondest memories? Where? When? Explain them.

Parents - Describe your parents. Mom and Dad. Home?
How was their health? Mental attitude?
What was your relationship with them?
What was their relationship with your children?
What were your feelings toward them at that phase of your life?

Siblings - How did your relationship with your siblings change or stay the same?
    Where did they live? Did you visit often?
    Were your families friendly?
    How did you feel about them?
    What is your fondest memory of them?

Married Life - Who was your spouse? Background?
    Describe your courtship and marriage.
    Describe personality, appearance, and why you chose him or her.
    How did your spouse enrich your life?
    What were the highlights of your life together?
    Would you marry that person again? Why or why not?
    How did you feel about marriage? Has your attitude changed?

Children - Names, birth dates, places of birth, etc.
    How did they enrich your life?
    How was each child different? Like you? (Need for achievement, appearance, personality, skills and problems)
    What are your fondest memories of them?
    How did you feel about them? Why?

Family Life - Were you happy with your family? Why? Why not?
    What activities did you share together?
    What stories did you tell your children? Add them.
    What are your fondest memories of them?
    How did you feel about the family?

Grandchildren - Names, parents, birth dates and homes?
    Write a story about your fondest memory of each one.
    Include appearance, personality, intelligence, abilities, skills, sense of humor.
    How did you feel about your grandchildren?

Appearance - How did your appearance change in adult life?
    (Weight, height, hair color, complexion)
    How did you feel about these changes?
    Did you take any measures to change your appearance?

Education - What and when did you attend college, post-graduate school, professional or trade school? Degree?
    What social skills did you learn?
    How did you feel about your education? How did it enrich your life?

Work Experience - How did you make a living? Tell about your job, titles, responsibilities, pay, positions, negatives, friends, and termination or retirement.
    How did you feel about your work? Would you choose it again? Why or why not? Was there time for family activities?

Personality Traits - What personality traits do you exhibit?
    Are they a detriment or asset?
    Where did they originate? How did you change them?
    How do you feel about your personality? Do you like yourself?

Character Traits - What character traits have you acquired in your adult life?
    Why and how did you change?
    Have they brought new happiness? Why? Why not?
    What character traits did you teach your children? (Honesty, respect)
    How did you feel about your character?

Intelligence - Do you think that you are intelligent? Why? Why not?
    Are you more intelligent in adult years?
    How do you feel about your intelligence?

Emotional Intelligence - Do you possess self-awareness, impulse control, persistence, zeal, self-motivation, empathy, social deftness and self-control?
    How do these qualities enrich your life?

Religious Activities - What religion are you? What role has it played in your life? What religious traditions do your practice? Is it your profession?
    How do you feel about religion?

Homes - Where did your family live? Description of home place and when you moved there. Explain your life style, friends and why your moved away.
    What was the surrounding environment?
    How did you feel about your homes?

Friends - Who were your adult friends? Did they live nearby?
    What activities did you enjoy? (Sports, movies, music)
    How did they enrich your life?
    How did you feel about friendships? Old and new ones?

Health - How did your health affect your happiness?
    Describe your health? (Problems, operations, diseases)
    How did you feel about your health? Were you a hypochondriac?

Social Activities - Are you a social being? What activities do you enjoy? (Dancing, lectures, parties, movies, dining out)
    Whom do you share them with?
    How do you feel about social activities?
    Would you prefer to stay home alone?

Hobbies - What is your favorite hobby? (Cooking, photography, cards, foreign films, board games, computers, model trains, stamps, reading, writing, sewing, TV)

How have they enriched your life? Emotionally? Financially?
How do you feel about hobbies and the role they play in your life?

Sports - Were you an athlete? Favorite sports? Why?
Teams you played on. Where? When? Memories of playing that sport.
Which sports do you watch on television?
Do you play individual or team sports? Describe your interest.
How do you feel about sports?

Music and Dance - Do you have rhythm? Is music your hobby?
What kind? (Classical, rock, opera, new wave, rap, show tunes, country western, jazz, Dixieland)
Do you play in an orchestra? What instrument? Where?
Do you dance? What kind of dancing do you enjoy?
How do you feel about music and dance?

The Arts - Are you artistic? Do you paint or draw?
Have you won any prizes? Who is your favorite artist? Why?
How do you feel about the arts?

Vacations - What vacations did you enjoy? Describe the places, people, climate, activities and feelings about them. Add photographs.

Food and Beverages - Do you enjoy cooking? What foods? Add recipes.
What were your favorite foods? Did you have special religious recipes?
What were the food fads then? What were your favorite beverages?
How did you feel about food and beverages?
Did you enjoy eating and drinking? Alone or with friends?

Holidays - How did you spend holidays? What traditions did you follow?
Did the family share them together?
Describe religious holidays, Fourth of July, Labor Day, birthdays, St. Patrick's Day, Columbus Day, Martin Luther King Day, Mother's Day, Father's Day, Valentine's Day, Thanksgiving, New Year's Eve, Memorial Day and other holidays.
What were your feelings about holidays?

Pets - What pets did you love? Names? Kinds? Describe them.
Were you a veterinarian?
How do you feel about animals and pets?

Politics - Were you a politician? What party? What was their platform?
Trace the party's history. (Origin, leaders, founders, changes)
How do you feel about politics?

History - How did your country's historical events affect your adult life? (The Great Depression, prohibition, war or peace, the 60s)
How did you feel about living in that era?

Problems - Did you have problems that interfered with your happiness? (Learning or physical disabilities, addiction, psychological disorders)
How did you solve your problems? (Therapy)
How did the problem affect your life?
How did you feel about these problems?

Milestones - What did you accomplish in these years?
How did you feel about these accomplishments?

Happy Times - What happy times do you remember? Describe them.
Why were they happy? Who shared your happiness?
How did you feel about them?

Sad Times - What sad times do you remember. Describe them.
Why were they sad? How did they change?
How did you feel about them?

Feelings - How did you feel about your adult life?
Describe your feelings.

Future Plans - What were your plans for the future?
Did you achieve them? How? When?

RETIREMENT
See page 98-110 for additional questions.

Memories - What are your fondest memories of your retirement?
Where did they take place? When? Describe them.
How did you feel about these memories?

Transition - How many years did you work? What professions?
Did you plan a semi retirement? How did it work out?
Did you enjoy your work? Why? Why not?
Were you successful? Financially? Emotionally?
Were you a workaholic? Why?
What was your attitude toward retirement?
What preparations did you make for retirement? (Financial, hobbies, new location, new skills and friends)
What goals did you plan to enjoy retirement? (Personal, educational, health, travel and volunteering)
How did you feel about retirement?

Parents - Are your parents alive? Where do they live? Do you visit them?
What is your relationship with them? How is their health?

Siblings - Do you enjoy a great relationship with them?

Where do they live? Do you visit them often?
What activities are you enjoying with them?
How do you feel about them?

Family Life - Is your family structure the same? (Wife and children)
Do you still have a mate, good health and adequate friends to enjoy your retirement years?
Have you had an easy adjustment to retirement?
How do you feel about your family life?

Children - Has your family remained the same?
Where do your children live? Have they changed?
Are they still in school? Do you see them often?
What is your relationship with them?
How do you feel about your children at this stage?
Are they a support and positive addition to your retirement years?

Grandchildren - Are your grandchildren living near you?
What are their names and ages?
Write stories about experiences with them.
Keep a diary of your impressions of them and their activities as they grow up. Add letters, photos, family stories, historical information about the times and a newspaper front page for every birthday. Give it to them for a birthday or graduation gift.
What stories do you tell about family legends and traditions? Record them. How do you feel about your grandchildren?

Appearance - How is your appearance changing? Remaining the same?
How do you solve these problems?
Do you exercise regularly? Are your attitudes positive?
What are your eating and drinking habits?
How do you feel about your appearance?

Health - How is your health? What are your problems?
How have they influenced your life style?
What is your mental attitude? Positive, enjoying life?
What plans have you made to insure your health? (Long term health care)
How do you feel about your health?

Economics - Did you plan for your retirement? Were you successful?
How did you plan for inflation? (Real estate investments, stocks, bonds)
Did you work to supplement your retirement?
What mistakes did you make planning for retirement?
How can they be changed?
How do you feel about your lifestyle in retirement?

Homes - Where are you living? Describe your home and surroundings?
Climate? Why did you choose this area?

How do you feel about your home?

Personality Traits - How has your personality remained the same? Changed?
For better or worse?
Have you gained or lost your sense of humor?
Are you becoming cynical and negative? Why?
How do you feel about your personality and how you relate to others?

Character Traits - What characteristic have you retained or acquired in your retirement years? Why? How?
How do you feel about your character?

Intelligence - Do you think that you are intelligent? What areas?
How is your memory? What activities do you do to preserve it?
(Crossword puzzles, exercise, writing, reading, conversation)

Emotional Intelligence - Do you possess self-awareness, have impulse control, persistence, zeal, self-motivation, empathy, social deftness and self-control?
What are you doing to acquire these traits?
How do these qualities enrich your life?
How do you feel about your emotional intelligence?

Religious Activities - What role does religion play in your retirement life?
Do you attend services regularly?
Do you volunteer at your place of worship?
Do you study your religion?
What religious traditions and holidays do you practice?
How do you feel about religion in your life?

Friends - Are you a social being? Do you enjoy people?
Do you have many friends? Describe them.
How do they enrich your life? What activities do you share with them?
How do you feel about friends?

Social Activities - What social activities do you enjoy? (Dancing, clubs, cards, games, dining out, lectures, travel)
Is your socializing confined to family events?
Whom do you share these activities with?
How do you feel about social activities or would you rather stay home and listen to classical music or read?

Hobbies - Writing your autobiography is a project. What other hobbies do you enjoy?
Have they changed in your retirement?
Why? Which ones have you added to your leisure time activities?
How do they enrich your life? Emotionally or financially?
How do you feel about hobbies?

Sports - What sports have you always enjoyed? Why?
   Which ones are new interests?
   Do you play individual or team sports? Why? Where? When?
   Do you watch sports on television? What is your favorite program?
   How do you feel about sports?

Music and Drama - Have you continued playing a musical instrument?
   Do you attend the symphony, ballet, opera or musicals?
   What kind of music do you enjoy? Why?
   Who is your favorite composer? Why?
   Has your taste in music changed? Why?
   What kind of dances do you enjoy? (Ballroom, country western)
   How do you feel about music and dance?

The Arts - Are you an artist? What do you draw, paint or sculpt?
   Have you studied? Where? When?
   Have you won any prizes? Where? When?
   Who is your favorite artist? Why?
   How do you feel about fine arts?

Holidays - How do you spend holidays? Alone or with family?
   What religious traditions do you follow?
   Describe religious holidays, Fourth of July, Labor Day, birthdays, St. Patrick's Day, Columbus Day, Martin Luther King Day, Mother's Day, Father's Day, Valentine's Day, Thanksgiving, New Year's Eve, Memorial Day and other holidays.
   What were your feelings about holidays?

Vacations - Describe the vacations that you have enjoyed. (Time, place, climate, people, experiences, sights and feelings) Add your journal notes.
   How do you feel about travel and vacations?

Pets - Do you have pets? Names? Kinds of animals?
   What role do they play in your life?
   How do you feel about your pets?

Politics - Are you interested and involved in politics? Where? Which party?
   Do you volunteer? How do you help?
   How have your political views changed?
   How do you feel about contemporary politics?

History - How are the country's historical events affecting your life style?
   How do you feel about the times you live in?

Changes - There have been many changes in your life (Death, loss of job, divorce). Describe them.
   How have you adjusted to them? Not adjusted?

Milestones - What have you accomplished in your retirement? (Climbed a mountain, took a trip alone or acquired a new skill) Explain. How do you feel about these experiences?

Happy Times - Describe your happiest times.
How did you make them happen?
Who was part of these experiences?
How do you feel about them?

Sad Times - What sad times have you experienced?
How did they happen? Could they be changed?
How do you feel abut them?

Feelings - How do you feel about retirement? Disappointed, sad or happy?

Evaluation of Life - Evaluate your life. Describe both your good and bad decisions.
When and why did you make mistakes?
What were the best decisions?
What do you attribute your happiness or sadness to? (Personality trait that led to poor choices, outside forces or other factors)
If you had your life to live over, how would you change it?
How do you feel about your life in general?

Future Plans - What are your future plans?
List ten goals and how you plan to make them a reality. (Learn a new language, write a book, climb a mountain, cruise around the world, build a house, paint a picture, learn to dance or get a college degree) Did you accomplish any of your previous goals? Explain how you made them a reality.

Katherine R. Berndes has a B.S. in Elementary Education and a M.A.L.S. in Education, Psychology and Anthropology from Wesleyan University, CT. She taught the writing process and has twenty-seven years experience in elementary, junior high and adult education.

The ideas in this book have been successfully implemented in her numerous autobiography classes in local schools, senior centers, and colleges.

She is a winner of the National League of American Pen Women local and national nonfiction, poetry and photography awards.